Six Sigma for Small Business

6σ SB Six Sigma for Small Business

Greg Brue
Six Sigma Consultants, Inc.

Ep Entrepreneur Press

Editorial Director: Jere Calmes
Cover Design: Beth Hanson-Winter

This is a CWL Publishing Enterprises book, developed and produced for
Entrepreneur Press by CWL Publishing Enterprises, Inc., Madison, Wisconsin,
www.cwlpub.com.

This publication is designed to provide accurate and authoritative information
in regard to the subject matter covered. It is sold with the understanding that
the publisher is not engaged in rendering legal, accounting, or other professional services. If legal advice or other expert assistance is required, the services
of a competent professional person should be sought.

—From a Declaration of Principles jointly adopted by
a Committee of the American Bar Association and
a Committee of Publishers and Associations

ISBN 1-932531-55-6

Library of Congress Cataloging-in-Publication Data
Brue, Greg.
  Six sigma for small business / by Greg Brue.
    p. cm.
  ISBN 1-932531-55-6 (alk. paper)
  1. Small business—Management. 2. Six sigma (Quality control standard)
I. Title.
  HD62.7.B79 2005
  658.4'013--dc22

                                                  2005019097

Printed in Canada

10 09 08 07 06 05   10 9 8 7 6 5 4 3 2 1

Contents

6σ
SB
Preface

Whoever admits that he is too busy to improve his methods has acknowledged himself to be at the end of his rope. And that is always the saddest predicament which anyone can get into.

—J. Ogden Armour

Six Sigma—you've heard of it, but it's for the big guys, right? Well, this book is here to refute that myth. What you need to understand is that, plain and simple, Six Sigma is a proven set of methods to help you run your business or organization more efficiently and profitably. It's a way to reduce waste, stop delivering defective products and services from inefficient processes, and make your customers more than satisfied. Jack Welch, the legendary former CEO of GE, called Six Sigma "the most important initiative GE has ever undertaken."

Why would he say that? The reason is that Six Sigma has increased GE's profitability dramatically. Scaling down the methods GE uses and applying them to small businesses is what you'll learn about in this book. You don't have to hire a staff of specialists to only do Six Sigma projects. You do, however, need to train and support your people in these efforts, giving them the time and resources needed to undertake and execute your Six Sigma improvement projects. In doing this, always keep in mind that you are not taking them away from "real work." Six Sigma improvement projects may just end up being the most important work they do. This is because Six Sigma projects aren't about dealing with the random problems that occur in your business from time to time. Don't look on your Six Sigma team as a bunch of firefighters. They are fire *preventers*. Their task is identify the most important causes of problems in your processes, whether they are on the shop floor or in the front office, and implement changes that will eliminate these problems *permanently*—to the benefit of everyone..

In *Six Sigma for Small Business*, I will systematically take you through this methodology. If you've never dealt with statistics and have mainly just dealt with problems as they arise, Six Sigma will seem a pretty drastic change from what you've been doing. But don't despair: anyone can master the steps in this improvement process and profit, often substantially, from doing so.

I want to warn you that it will take some effort and commitment to learn Six Sigma. There is some math involved, though I've worked hard to keep it basic and appropriate to the kinds of problems small business managers are likely to confront. There are also various graphs and other tools involved to help identify, understand, and take on the problems that will deliver the most improvement for the effort expended. That's the whole point of Six Sigma: fixing the problems that will have the greatest payoff in terms of cost savings, improved customer satisfaction, and profit.

There's something else you need to understand about Six Sigma and why it makes sense for small business. By involving your employees in improvement projects through the Six Sigma methodology, you are improving their skills and giving them a sense of empowerment. This naturally leads to higher motivation and commitment to your success because it is their own as well. Of course, this also assumes that you are committed to properly implementing Six Sigma in your organization and provide your employees with what they need to succeed.

This is an important point: Six Sigma is not a quick-fix or flavor-of-the-month management fad. It's based on using science and an established set of steps that will give you the bottom-line results you and your employees want.

About This Book

One of my goals is to engage you and keep you interested as you proceed through the book. To that end, nearly every chapter starts off with a story of some small business and how Six Sigma could have helped or did help that business to grow and become more profitable. So look for those and consider how they might relate to your operations.

Chapter 1 gives you a basic overview of what this Six Sigma stuff is all about and why it's become so well accepted in thousands of businesses in the U.S. and around the world. It will get you thinking about some areas where you might undertake Six Sigma improvement projects.

Chapter 2 talks about quality and its place in management. You'll read about how intiating Six Sigma will affect your employees and what your role is in all this. I touch briefly on Six Sigma and company culture, but I want to emphasize here as well that developing a culture that supports your Six Sigma efforts is vital to your success. So keep that in mind as you read and decide how to use Six Sigma in your business.

To be able to improve something, you have to know how to measure it. **Chapter 3** provides a brief overview of some useful business metrics and how to use them to your advantage. Metrics help you understand what's going right and where you can make improvements. I also introduce some basic—very basic—statistics in this chapter, which are vital to creating and interpreting the metrics that will be most useful to you in identifying improvement projects and measuring your results.

Chapter 4 is all about the people who will be involved in your Six Sigma initiative. Over time, especially influenced by GE's approach, different roles have emerged—Champions, Black Belts, Green Belts, Project Team Members—and the people who take on these roles are responsible for executing Six Sigma projects in your company. This chapter gives you a clear description of these roles so you think about which of your people would be best suited to them.

Picking an improvement project on which to unleash the power of Six Sigma is an important consideration, and this is what you'll learn about in **Chapter 5**. Here you'll read about key criteria for selecting a project with the most payoff. You'll also learn what bad projects are and how to avoid selecting those. You'll learn about a tool, Pareto charts, that will help you drill down into a problem to identify which factors are the most important in terms of costs vs. benefits.

The Six Sigma methodology is structured into five phases—Define, Measure, Analyze, Improve, and Control (DMAIC). **Chapters 6-10**, one chapter at a time, take you through each of these steps and how to apply them to small business problems. This five-step process is logical and, in fact, even intuitive. All Six Sigma does is apply it with discipline and tools that allow you and your employees to systematically maximize results.

Chapter 6 explains the *Define* phase. Here you'll learn about how to define your problem in a way that allows everyone to clearly understand it in terms of why it was chosen and what the potential savings will be from finding its causes and eliminating them.

The second phase in the Six Sigma process is *Measure*, and that's the topic of **Chapter 7**. You've defined the problem, now you have to measure, using metrics discussed in Chapter 3 and different tools, how the inputs into your processes are causing outcomes that keep your business from being more effective. In other words, you establish relationships between what you do and what's going wrong.

Once you've established those relationships, you're ready for the *Analyze* phase, the subject of **Chapter 8**. Here you learn how to develop a hypothesis about which inputs are most closely related to the problems you're experiencing so you can make changes that will result in the improvements you seek.

Now we reach what some might call the action step: the *Improve* phase, covered in **Chapter 9**. Here's where you test your hypothesis and see if the changes you're considering will actually work. The Improve phase helps you establish real correlations between inputs and outputs and create experiments that will determine which changes will give you the results you're looking for—results that make it all worthwhile. This chapter is a bit more demanding some of the others, but that's the nature of this methodology. It's logical and scientific, but it also requires that, through experiments, you make the right changes. So keep that in mind as you work through this chapter.

Finally, you've made the changes and gotten the gains you hoped for. The final step in the process is the *Control* phase, **Chapter 10**. This is where you ensure that the changes you've made will be sustained, with even more improvements possible. In this chapter you'll get introduced to control charts and how to use them to keep your processes working well and to quickly deal with issues that may arise.

So that's it—Six Sigma for your small business. There is a final chapter, however. **Chapter 11** is a brief one on taking stock of what you've learned and how you can begin implementing Six Sigma in your business. If your company is large enough to use a Six Sigma consultant, I give you some advice on choosing one who will meet your needs. I also include case studies that show how DMAIC worked in three companies to get outstanding results.

There you have it. Thanks for choosing this book—and good luck as you embark on your Six Sigma journey!

Acknowledgments

This book is a collaboration, and I want to acknowledge the important help I received in its development. This is the fourth book I've worked on with John Woods and his company, CWL Publishing Enterprises, Inc., a book packaging company in Madison, Wisconsin. Without their help this book wouldn't have happened. While John keeps me motivated and Nancy Woods serves as proofreader, the editor at CWL, Bob Magnan, is as much responsible for the final product you see here as anyone. He's tough, but his efforts are visible on every page. I am happy to have worked with them on all my book projects and thank them for their friendship and continued help. One more person I want to thank is Dan John for making the final edits prior to sending the manuscript to CWL. I also want to thank my wife, Kelly, who read and edited several chapters and has helped in ways that go beyond what you see on the page.

Greg Brue is the world's leading practitioner of the Six Sigma methodology and an original Six Sigma pioneer. Greg worked in concert with Jack Welch and Larry Bossidy catapulting the success of the unprecedented GE and Allied Signal initiatives. His success model and training content have been regarded as the standard in the industry for over a decade. Greg has authored and contributed to numerous articles that have appeared in international business publications such as *Strategy & Business*, *The Russian Journal*, *Globiz*, *The CEO Refresher*, *The American Banker*, *The Manufacturer*, and *Inside Quality*. He is also author of the bestselling *Six Sigma for Managers*. His dynamic style has also made him a favored key-note speaker for business conferences and major industry events. He holds positions as an Executive Professor at Texas A&M University Center for Retail Studies, the Kellogg School of Management, and Wake Forest University MBA program. Visit his Web site at **www.sixsigmaco.com**.

6σ
SB

Chapter 1
What Is Six Sigma and Why Should I Care?

The toughest thing about success is that
you've got to keep on being a success.
—Irving Berlin

Nearly bankrupt ... and I've only been open three months. My name is Tom Little, and I'm a recovering Six Sigma skeptiholic. A seasoned business owner who has been around the block a few times, my career has run the gamut from top secret government research, design engineering, to C-level executive management—credentials that have carried me through countless opportunities and business scenarios.

My small business adventure begins like most I guess, with barriers along the way that most of you who run small businesses know about. It ends with a lesson in humility that has become the single most important lesson of my career: You don't know what you don't know. My pitfall was my overconfidence, arrogance if you will, in my pedigree and ability to tackle the common problems every business is plagued with.

Much of my career has been spent living in airports, and I will do anything to make that as hassle-free as possible. I had seen a few other airports with valet parking and wanted to bring this convenience to my city, if only to fulfill my own selfish agenda. I created and then pitched my business plan for this service to city officials who embraced my idea and offered me a pilot program. Jackpot! Yep, I had a winner and once my venture hit the newspaper, others who wanted to provide this service appeared out of nowhere wanting to be the exclusive provider of these services at our airport. Yes this was an international airport, but was there enough business for more than one valet service? No! City officials therefore were left with no option but to put the service out for bid. My victory was short-lived but long enough that I had purchased a building and parking lot, hired a staff and leased vans. I was in deep, and the delays of the bid process and associated red tape drained my cash reserve. (Navigating the bureaucracy of city government was a painful task, and I caution you to do your homework before jumping into this game.)

I was the low bidder and being awarded the contract was anti-climactic. I started moving forward and launched a marketing campaign and started parking cars.

Three months into my new business venture I was faced with closing my doors. Staffing and labor were eating into the profit causing a negative cash flow to my already drained reserves. The problem was staffing correctly without adversely affecting the wait time of the customers. The principal reason for the airport valet service was convenience. Get the customers' cars to them in a short time, with additional services (car wash, oil change), at a small premium over the traditional park and ride.

My good idea along with my enthusiasm were being squelched. All I wanted to do was provide a valuable service to the community and make some money doing it.

As they say, desperate times call for desperate measures.

I had a friend who received Six Sigma training through his company, and we would occasionally get into debates over this "quality fad" designed for big businesses. Being at the end of my rope, I presented the problem to my friend expecting to hear some complicated jargon with no real solution. I sat there for the first five minutes listening to him thinking yeah, yeah, yeah. But the more he talked the more I realized there was no disputing the method he was describing. I was shocked, and if it weren't for my curiosity to see more, I would have crawled in a hole. What he was explaining to me sounded simple. He solved my problem in 15 minutes. First he asked me to define what the problems were with specific numbers not anecdotal statements. The moment of epiphany came from one specific question. "What are staffing requirements a function of? Is it the airline scheduling?" Duh! I should use the airline schedule to set up a pattern of peak traffic times, and low traffic times to directly drive our staffing needs, use part-time trained floaters to work the peak, and full time key staff to open, close, and maintain the average capacity of the business. That was it! The simple relationship of staffing to airline schedule was going to put me into the profit zone.

Converted and thirsty for more, I signed up for training in Six Sigma and learned that the real power comes from applying it to all key issues instead of using it to fight fires.

My life and outlook is changed along with my approach to business. I had found out that Six Sigma is not a fad, nor is it just for the *Fortune* 500. Six Sigma is a simple, practical problem-solving tool for any size business.

My Six Sigma friend quoted a line from General Eric Shinseki, the former chief of staff of the U.S. Army, that I will never forget and remind myself of daily: "If you hate change then you're going to like irrelevance even less."

Welcome to Six Sigma

Welcome to *Six Sigma for Small Business*! You are about to embark on an exciting journey that will allow you to improve your profits, uncover hidden waste and costs in your business, eliminate complacency, and increase overall quality and customer satisfaction. Take this Six Sigma journey with the same passion you did in getting your business started, and you will reap the rewards.

Six Sigma has been widely adopted by American businesses because it works! I have been in the trenches implementing the Six Sigma improvement methodology in major corporations since 1994, and I have seen incredible results over and over again. You, the small business owner, can achieve these same amazing breakthroughs by applying Six Sigma to your organization.

This book is designed for small business owners and managers who want to learn how the Six Sigma problem-solving and improvement methodology can help solve immediate business problems and who are ready to take advantage of the gains that Six Sigma can bring them.

How much do you know about Six Sigma? Maybe you've heard of it, but you're not sure what it is. Or, perhaps you think you know what it is, but you can't imagine how it would apply to your small business like it has been applied at a giant company like GE. Then again, maybe you've never heard of Six Sigma but you would like to learn about this problem-solving methodology because you want to improve your business. In other words, regardless of your level of Six Sigma knowledge, if you own a small business and want it to make breakthrough improvements in terms of efficiency, cost savings, customer satisfaction, and profitability, this book is for you.

In other words, this book is for you if:

- You want to turn your current mistakes into profit. (Note: you can't turn mistakes into dollars. You can however, get rid of mistakes and realize lower costs and improved performance and profitability as a result.)
- You want more time for a personal life.
- Your business is doing well, but you know it could do much, much better.
- You want to increase profit.
- You want to make a better product/service at lower cost with less waste and rework.
- You want to deliver higher quality services and products to your customers.
- You want to increase the satisfaction of your customers.
- You want to grow and expand your business.
- You want to maximize your employees' contribution and increase their level of commitment.

- You want to make more money!

"Show me the money!" the star football player screamed in the movie *Jerry Maguire*. And showing you the money is the natural outcome of Six Sigma. This happens because you'll run your business more efficiently while at the same time you'll be enhancing the commitment of your employees and making your customers happier.

Defining Six Sigma and Starting on the Path

What is Six Sigma? To put it very simply, Six Sigma is a problem-solving methodology that reduces costs and improves customer satisfaction by greatly reducing waste in all the processes involved in the creation and delivery of your products and/or services.

More specifically, Six Sigma is a problem-solving technology that uses data, measurements, and statistics to identify the *vital few* factors that will dramatically decrease waste and defects while increasing predictable results, customer satisfaction, profit, and shareholder value.

Six Sigma is about data and facts, and *not* about thinking, feeling, or believing what you conceive to be the solution to the problem. As Sergeant Joe Friday said on the TV show *Dragnet*, "Just the facts, ma'am."

> **Sigma** A term used in statistics that measures standard deviation. In business, it is an indication of defects in the outputs of a process and how far these outputs deviate from perfection.
>
> **Six Sigma** A statistical concept that measures a process in terms of defects. At the six sigma level, there are only 3.4 defects per million opportunities. Six Sigma is also a philosophy of managing that focuses on eliminating defects through practices that emphasize understanding, measuring, and improving processes.

The elementary Six Sigma methodology was developed, tested, and proven at Motorola in the early 1980s. I had the privilege of being one of the six original pioneers who created what is now simply called "Six Sigma." After it was proven at Motorola, other companies began to adopt this methodology. First it was Allied Signal. General Electric was then the

> **Vital few** The "vital few" is a recurring concept in Six Sigma. In this context, it refers to the main actions or events in a process that cause problems. By dealing with these vital few causes, we can often dramatically reduce problems. Six Sigma helps us identify the vital few and then provides a step-by-step methodology for process improvement.

next company to adopt Six Sigma, with unprecedented success. Jack Welch, former CEO of GE, credits Six Sigma with increasing the gap between GE and any close competitor. I was there and knew Jack Welch was a self-proclaimed cynic when it came to quality-type programs, but this is what he said about Six Sigma: "I describe Six Sigma as the most important initiative GE has ever undertaken."

Just as Six Sigma invigorated GE, it can do the same for your organization. It is a myth that Six Sigma only works for large companies. GE treated its business as many small business units integrated together. In this book I will share the technology of Six Sigma and teach you how to apply it to your business. I will break down the elements of Six Sigma and put them into simple terms so that you can directly implement this methodology in your everyday business processes, immediately. Even if you've never taken a business course, you will be able to utilize the concepts, terminology, and methods presented in this book to achieve Six Sigma success.

The Six Sigma journey begins with an understanding of some of its most basic components.

The Basic Components of Six Sigma

There are three basic concepts that are common to all businesses that Six Sigma addresses: processes, defects, and variation. You may not have used these terms before, but let's look at each one.

Process

A fundamental concept of Six Sigma is *process*. A process is any set of repetitive steps—in any manufacturing, services, or transactional environment to achieve some result. There are processes for all of your core business activities and functions. They are the steps that the people in your organization go through to do their jobs and deliver your products or services. You may not have thought much about them, but they're there nevertheless. Understanding them and making them work at the highest level possible is the goal of Six Sigma.

Defects

Part of the Six Sigma methodology includes measuring a process in terms of defects. Six Sigma helps you eliminate those defects so you can consistently and profitably produce and deliver products or services that meet

> **Process** Any repetitive steps—in a transactional, manufacturing, or services environment to achieve some result. The Six Sigma methodology collects data on variations in outputs associated with each process, so that the process can be improved and those variations reduced.
>
> **Examples**
> - Steps you take in billing your customers
> - Taking customer orders
> - Fulfilling customer orders

and exceed your customers' expectations. It's not unusual for a small business to have a minimum of 10 percent of its net income being wasted by process defects. In other words, those defects are dollars wasted!

Here are typical defects we have all experienced:

- Scheduling defect at doctor's office
- Waiting in line at drive-through (wrong food, too much time)

> **Defect** A measurable characteristic of the process or its output that is not within acceptable customer limits, in other words, not conforming to specifications. The sigma level of a process is calculated in terms of the number of *defects* in ratio to the number of *opportunities* for defects.
>
> **Examples**
> - Getting someone else's dry cleaning order
> - Waiting for more than five minutes in the fast food drive-through line
> - Shipping damage
> - Incorrect invoices
> - Missed deadlines
>
> Anything with the prefix of "re" such as rework, rebill, rethink, redo, resend, reconstruct, rebuild, reprocess, re-paint, reestablish, recover, resolve, recondition, rewash, rewrite, resubmit, renegotiate, repropose, revisit, return etc. You get the point!

- Waiting too long to get the restaurant bill
- Not getting paid on time
- Bank statement errors
- Telephone bill errors
- E-mail errors
- Car wash not completely cleaning your car
- Dry cleaning spots on your clothes
- Hardware store out of the single item you need
- Pricing errors at your local retail store
- Product defects making you return items back to retailer or manufacturer
- Your spouse not remembering your anniversary (or was that you?)

The list can go on for the remainder of this book, but the point here is that these are everyday life defects, and businesses have defect lists just as long and, in some cases, interact with your personal defect list.

Variation

The Six Sigma methodology reduces variations in business processes. It seems obvious, but you can't consistently produce a high quality product or service (your output) if you have variations in your processes, right?

> **Variation** Any quantifiable difference between a specified measurement or standard and the deviation from such measurements or standard in the output of a process. Variation in outputs can result from many causes in the functioning and management of processes.

Basically, you have achieved six sigma when your processes deliver only 3.4 defects per million opportunities (DPMO). For example, this would mean that out of one million bags checked in at the airport luggage counter, only 3.4 would be lost. In other words, your processes are working almost perfectly. Of course, this is very difficult to do, but you can begin to approach it (or at least get a lot better) by implementing the methods described in this book. The fact is that most businesses operate at three to four sigma quality levels, which translates to about 25 percent of their revenue lost to defects in their processes. Those defects represent waste, rework, higher costs, and dissatisfied customers. At what level of quality level does your business operate? Wouldn't you like to do better? Of course you would! That's what this book is all about.

Now that you have a preliminary understanding of the basic concepts of Six Sigma, you may be asking "Can Six Sigma really work for a small business?" The answer is, Six Sigma can be implemented in any business, regardless of what you do or how small you are. Six Sigma is about problem-solving, and problems are everywhere. It doesn't matter what type or size of business this breakthrough methodology is applied to. You might be a wholesaler, a retailer, a manufacturer, or a service organization. You might have three employees, or maybe you have 300. No matter, Six Sigma will work for you.

Common Myths About Six Sigma

Over the years I have talked to hundreds of business leaders, and I could not possibly count or include here the number of misconceptions I have heard about Six Sigma. However, here are some of the most common myths about Six Sigma:

- It applies only to large companies.
- It only works in manufacturing settings. Although it's true that Six Sigma started in manufacturing, it has been applied successfully in all segments of business—banking, healthcare, the military, fast-food chains, airlines, hotels, retail stores, and on and on and on. If there's a repetitive process with a problem, you can apply Six Sigma!
- You must hire an outside consultant.
- You need experts (i.e., "Black Belts"), to make it work.
- Six Sigma is a complicated, statistical methodology that the ordinary person is incapable of understanding.
- Six Sigma doesn't include customer requirements. That's totally false. Every Six Sigma project starts with the customers, with determining the factors that are critical to the customer. Those factors focus the project.

- Six Sigma is repackaged Total Quality Management. Quality programs are valuable in that they can create a quality perspective and culture. But Six Sigma fixes identifiable, chronic problems that directly impact your bottom line. Six Sigma projects are selected to reduce or eliminate waste, which translates into lower costs, happier customers and real money for the bottom line. Six Sigma is not theory. It defines, measures, analyzes, improves, and controls the vital few processes that matter most, to tie quality improvement directly to bottom-line results.

- Six Sigma is an accounting game without real savings.

- Six Sigma is just training.

- Six Sigma is a "magic pill" to fix problems with little effort.

If you feel intimidated by the idea of adopting the Six Sigma methodology or you are in any way unsure of your ability to succeed at it, I can assure you that you're not alone. Every business leader I have ever worked with has felt the same way you do at the beginning. But once you understand and recognize what Six Sigma can achieve for your organization, it's easy to embrace it with enthusiasm. Let's address some of the concerns you might have and get them out of the way—they are roadblocks on your journey to Six Sigma success.

Common Concerns About Implementing Six Sigma

Fear of Change. It makes sense that if you're going to improve the way your business functions you're going to have to make some changes, some of them major. But, many people are afraid of change. Nevertheless, while we might feel comfortable doing the same things every day, this means we will just keep making the same mistakes over and over. In other words, if you're not willing to change how you do some things in your business, you won't be able to *improve* your business.

Fear of Commitment. Again, this is a common problem for many people. It's true that to reach the gains that Six Sigma can produce, you have to be dedicated to it. At the risk of sounding like a cliché, anything worth having is worth working for, right? You've undoubtedly been extremely committed to the success of your business. Six Sigma requires a high level of commitment, as well.

Fear of Disruption. Ok, things may not be going as well as you'd like business-wise, but at least it works! In other words, why fix it if it ain't broke (or at least completely broken)? Well, your business may be doing just fine, but it can do better. You can make your customers happier, you can produce a better product or service, you can reduce costs, and you can make higher profits!

Increased Cost. Implementing Six Sigma or any new program is going to cost me money and I'm not sure it will be worth the cost. This is a reasonable concern, but if you do it properly, you can be sure that you will decrease, not increase, your costs.

Wasted Time Without Results. Maybe you've tried other programs to make your operations more efficient and after a while these just didn't work. This is valid, but this shouldn't be a problem with Six Sigma. It's aimed at specific problems with a specific problem-solving methodology, with the goal of eliminating forever that problem.

All of these fears and concerns are valid. After all, no one likes the idea of getting out of his or her comfort zone.

But if you *know* that you will not be able to overcome these concerns, then this book is not for you, and neither is Six Sigma.

As Sam Walton, the founder of Wal-Mart, once said, "High expectations are the key to everything." We all know where Sam Walton's high expectations led him! As a small business owner, you must constantly reach for more—complacency is your enemy. The fact that you bought this book is proof that you want to improve your business, but I can't emphasize enough that to succeed with Six Sigma you must be dedicated to it. But that won't necessarily be so hard once you begin to see the results. Let's move on.

You may be wondering at this point what *exactly* can Six Sigma do for you? Why should you do it? Here's the bottom line.

Six Sigma Will Help You to:

- Identify hidden waste and costs
- Identify and eliminate defects
- Increase profit margins
- Increase customer satisfaction
- Increase your employees' satisfaction and level of commitment
- Grow and expand your business

Let's briefly elaborate on these benefits.

1. **Identify hidden waste and costs:** On a personal level, if I ask you to give me the last two years of your check register, do you think I could find some waste? And are there hidden or natural spending patterns that *don't* need to exist?

2. **Identify and eliminate defects:** In your business do you ever have to spend effort and money on FedEx sending things overnight that should not have to be FedEx-ed due mainly to your poor planning or some other related defect caused by your internal process?

3. **Increase profit margins:** How can you increase profit in your business? There are typically two ways: 1) increase the price of the services or product you are selling, or 2) decrease the cost of goods/services. This means you either need a differentiator to increase your price or to decrease the cost of goods and services you *must* identify and fix the defects that raise your costs.

4. **Increase customer satisfaction:** For the small business owner, this benefit should probably be at the top of this list. After all, your main function is to make your customers happy and keep them wanting to do business with you. Companies exist for one purpose: to profitably serve customers. So it follows that any problem-solving initiative should help you do that. (See sidebar on next page for more on this.)

5. **Increase your employees' satisfaction and level of commitment:** Your people and you can enjoy solving a problem that costs you time and money. Employees feel like owners when they have the tools and are allowed to fix costly problems in the business. It provides a great sense of accomplishment for everyone.

> ### What Exactly Is Customer Satisfaction?
>
> The *customer* is a *person*, not an organization, business, or corporation. Your customer is a human being with needs, wants, and problems, just like you. *Satisfaction* is the extent of *certainty* a person has that his or her standards will be met by the product or service you provide. As certainty increases, the likelihood of satisfaction increases as well.
>
> Customers have what are termed "critical-to-quality," or CTQ, expectations. (CTQ is an important Six Sigma concept.) These CTQ expectations are important to understand and help assure that you will satisfy your customers. For example, what are the CTQs for a customer at McDonald's? 1) Waited on quickly. 2) Take order courtesously. 3) Order is correct and food is fresh. 4) Food is consitent with expectations for McDonald's.

6. **Grow and expand your business:** "Growth," like any other problem, is a problem to solve. So what are the market factors to grow and expand? Is your business ignoring a distribution channel, or perhaps the Internet is not being used effectively. What are the most important factors for growth? What is your growth objective for this year? Six Sigma is about asking new questions and then systematically finding answers.

I want you to stop here for a minute and think about your business. After all, this book is about how Six Sigma can benefit *you*. The following exercise is designed to help you become more familiar with how your business operates and the problems you may be experiencing. It will also get you into the Six Sigma mode of thinking.

Finding Your Areas of Improvement

The following exercise will help get you thinking about areas you can improve in your business.

1. Six Sigma is a *problem-solving* methodology. List four problems your business is experiencing right now.

   _____

   _____

   _____

   _____

2. Now think about the day-to-day operations of your organization. List four of your major repetitive processes.

    _____

    _____

    _____

    _____

3. Next, think about the defects affecting your product(s) or service(s), or outputs. What four defects do you see on a regular basis? List them below.

    _____

    _____

    _____

    _____

4. Finally, what variations do you see in your business processes? Variations, for example, might include differences in the way you do things from day to day or in your outputs. List the four major variations below.

    _____

    _____

    _____

    _____

Now you're starting to get the concepts, and this is the initial list for targeting areas of improvement and identifying the business problems that can keep you up at night. Keep this list handy, as we will use it in the coming chapters to start problem solving

Summary

When you can identify and quantify hidden process defects, you can eliminate them and move those wasted dollars to the bottom line and to investment in new opportunities to grow your business. By knowing which factors affect your process outputs and cause problems, you can take the steps to improve them. Gaining and using that knowledge is the goal of Six Sigma.

Like peeling an onion, Six Sigma uncovers the layers of process variables and defects that you need to understand and control to eliminate the wasted time, effort, and materials that add to your costs but don't add value for your customers. It's a problem-solving technology, but it's also a management methodology that ties process improvement directly to lowered costs, improved customer satisfaction, and higher returns on your investment of time and money in your business. Six Sigma is far more than a "quality" fad. The proof? Hundreds of companies are implementing Six Sigma as you are reading this book. They are lowering their costs, improving customer satisfaction, and increasing their profit. In other words, they are getting great results. Now you can as well!

6σ SB | Chapter 2
Six Sigma, Your Business, and You

Mistakes are the portals of discovery.
—James Joyce

Here is an ultimately sad story about a small plumbing business and the "Six Sigma Plumber." It was late one night before I was scheduled to travel out of town. It was raining unusually hard. I couldn't sleep and decided to check on the house for any problems due to the rain. When I opened the basement door, the water was up to the fifth step, with boxes and other things floating around. I had a major flood on my hands! It was 1:00 a.m. and I was leaving in a few hours for an important meeting that could not be delayed. I knew the sump pump wasn't working. I decided to call a 24-hour plumber to fix the problem.

This Six Sigma Plumber was amazing! He asked a few questions on the phone to help him diagnose the problem. I asked him to be as quiet as possible to avoid waking my wife, our two small sons, and our dog. He got to the house in only 35 minutes. He approached the house in a truck with the headlights off. He didn't ring the doorbell because I had the door open ready to greet him. He took off his boots and rolled out a rug to wipe his socks off. He then put on a pair of tall waterproof boots. He set up three large pumps from the truck to remove the water from the basement. By 3:00 a.m. he had replaced the sump pump to eliminate the remaining water. He quietly set aside items that needed to dry and turned on two heated fans to air-dry the basement. He gathered his tools, wiped his socks off, rolled up his rug, and left at 3:30 a.m. No one woke up. He sent me his bill and I paid it. The Six Sigma Plumber delivered the highest-quality service and I was a very satisfied customer.

So, why is this a sad story? Because in this world of so-called quality, customer expectations are so low that companies like this are rare. Why was I excited to get what I paid for? Because typically we get a lot less!

My entire experience with that small plumbing company was consistent from the phone call to the billing. Six Sigma reflects a quality throughout the entire business.

Here's an interesting activity that will really open your eyes about the problems plaguing small businesses. Open the Yellow Pages for your area and you will find thousands of small businesses with hundreds of thousands of defects. Let's briefly browse through the Pages, beginning with listings under "A," and identify just a few defects you might be familiar with:

- **Accountants**—Has an accountant ever prepared your income tax returns incorrectly? Did you have to pay penalties?

- **Advertising and Media**—Have you ever spent too much for advertising without the return you expected on your investment? Don't you wish you could get that money back?

- **Automobiles**—Have you ever had a dissatisfying experience at your local car dealership? Is there anyone out there who hasn't? Let's move on to the B's.

- **Banks**—Have you ever gone to an ATM to withdraw cash from your bank account and the machine ate your card? Or maybe you drove all over town and couldn't find an ATM that worked at all?

- **Beauty**—Have you or your spouse ever received a bad haircut or color at a beauty salon?

- **Burglar Alarms**—Has your home or business security alarm ever malfunctioned? Why does it always seem to happen in the middle of the night?

Let's skip to the R's.

- **Real Estate**—Has an agent ever shown you homes completely out of your price range or located in an undesirable area, wasting your time?

- **Restaurants**—Have you ever been served a lukewarm plate of pasta or a wilted salad? Have you ever gotten food poisoning?

- **Roofers**—Have you ever had your roof repaired, only to have it leak soon after? Or, maybe you waited all day, but the roofer never showed up?

You get the idea—there are defects everywhere! Imagine the amount of money those defects represent to the owners of these businesses. Do you think they would like to eliminate those defects? Do you think they'd like to improve the quality of their products or services and make their customers happier?

> **Quality** The degree or grade of excellence of a product or service and how well it meets or exceeds customer expectations.

Let's take a closer look at the broad concept of *quality*—something that most people think about in abstract, general terms. What exactly is "quality"?

A Very Brief History of the Quality Movement

Up until the 1950s, businesses around the world functioned in pretty much the same way: they focused on mass production, on *quantity*. After World War II, W. Edwards Deming helped the Japanese to revitalize their industries by focusing on *quality*. His approach became known as Total Quality Management (TQM)—a term that Deming never liked. He just saw this as a more intelligent way to get better results, an approach that reduced costs, improved customer satisfaction, and facilitated greater growth and profitability.

Because of the phenomenal success of the Japanese industries, U.S. businesses started to take a serious look at TQM. By the 1980s, many business leaders began to see Deming's point that the use of statistics, teamwork, and process control would lead to continuous improvement, higher quality, and lower costs. Those companies that adopted TQM underwent major changes: *quality* became the focus and the name of the game.

> **Total Quality Management (TQM)** A management approach that views a business as a system consisting of teams and processes. It focuses on company-wide continuous improvement and producing and delivering products and services that meet or exceed customer expectations.

By the mid-1980s, however, some in the business community had become impatient and disenchanted with TQM. Continuous improvement is worthwhile, of course, but it wasn't producing the great financial results that many had expected. The solution? Six Sigma. This was not a rejection of TQM, but a refinement of it to introduce a methodology for achieving results more systematically.

The Six Sigma methodology was initially developed at Motorola because technology was becoming so complex that long-held views about acceptable quality levels were no longer adequate. In 1989 Motorola set a five-year goal: a defect rate of 3.4 parts per million—a quality level of six sigma, essentially as near perfection as you can get in terms of process outputs. The success of Motorola's Six Sigma initiative changed American concepts of quality and the means of measuring it. Other companies noticed and the Six Sigma revolution took hold.

You've probably heard about TQM or at least quality assurance is part of your business model. But although Six Sigma is a disciplined extension of TQM, Six Sigma is more focused; I like to use the term "surgical." Six Sigma concentrates on the *vital few* processes—those that contribute the most to the costs of products and services and to the quality of outputs. It uses business metrics to identify those vital few processes, *connecting quality to cost and the bottom line.* This is how Six Sigma generates profit.

Defining Quality for Small Business

Quality for the small business doesn't mean the same thing as for a large organization. Why not? Well, the key difference has to do with size. A large company, with a variety of products or services and lots of resources (like cash), can sometimes afford to provide its customers with less than high quality and still stay in business.

For example, there are big retailers that offer a wide variety of quality goods at competitive prices, but provide poor customer service. Regardless, consumers continue to shop in their stores because of the low prices—they're willing to put up with poor quality service to get those prices.

I'll go even further and state that customers have actually come to *expect* lower quality from large corporations, as long as the corporations make up for it in other ways. We expect some defects. Here are some examples to illustrate this point:

- Cell phone companies drop calls.
- Car manufacturers recall millions of vehicles.
- Home appliances need constant repairs and/or extended warranties.
- Airlines lose luggage.

When defects like these rear their ugly heads, are we surprised? Of course not. And, more often than not, these defects do not prevent us from continuing to patronize these businesses because we derive other benefits from them that mean more to us. For example, maybe your cell phone company drops calls, but you got a great deal on it from that company. Or, your car might have been recalled, but it gets great gas mileage. And, although you had to buy an extended warranty on that dishwasher, it's the quietest one on the market. Finally, even though the airline lost your luggage, it had the best deals on Disney vacation packages! You see what I mean.

On the other hand, it's entirely different for the small business. In most cases, a small business can't overcome defects in quality. The bottom line: defects will slowly kill you. They will put you out of business. Do you agree? If not, you're in denial. If you don't eliminate defects, your customers will go elsewhere. You can use Six Sigma to get rid of those defects once and for all! And the fact is that maybe your competitors will be using Six Sigma.

I have been trying to sell you on the benefits of Six Sigma. I hope I have succeeded. But before we move on to actually learning how to do it, I want you to pause for a moment and consider the human element of Six Sigma.

Six Sigma is all about identifying and fixing problems that lower costs, improve quality, and raise your bottom line. But businesses are about more than just money; businesses are *people*. So what are the internal effects of Six Sigma? How will Six Sigma affect your employees and your company's culture?

Six Sigma and Your Employees

If you want to maximize your employees' contributions and commitment to your business, you should do Six Sigma. But why does Six Sigma motivate employees?

The answer is simple: Six Sigma inspires employees because it gives them the opportunity to make a difference—by giving them the tools to better understand their own work processes and to make decisions about how to improve them. In a Six Sigma deployment, every single employee, regardless of his or her position in the company hierarchy, is vitally important. Each employee is encouraged to provide input and participate in the company's initiative to improve quality, meet or exceed customer expectations, cut costs, and improve the bottom line. And, each employee owns his or her part of the process to be improved. In other words, it really is a *team* effort.

Empowerment is a great, feel-good concept. But can we measure it? Look at Figure 2-1 and consider your employees. How empowered are they?

Are your employees fully engaged? Are they emotionally and intellectually connected to the organization? Are they actively involved? Will they be supportive of change?

0 Sigma	A lowly slug. You have no grade point.
.1 Sigma	I will tell you what to do next.
.2 Sigma	You will ask what to do next.
.5 Sigma	Bring me your problems.
1 Sigma	Bring me your problems with your ideas.
2 Sigma	Bring me your problems with your recommendations.
3 Sigma	Bring me your problems with your recommendations. If you don't hear from me, just proceed.
4 Sigma	Take action

Figure 2-1. A possible scale of empowerment related to Six Sigma

When a company is deeply committed to changing how it functions and improving its processes, employees willingly go along and give their best effort. Six Sigma energizes people. And let's face it: your employees are fully aware of your company's problems and defects and frustrated by them. They'd like to fix them almost as much as you would!

There's another element to employee motivation—compensation. Many companies tie bonuses, raises, and even promotions to the success of their Six Sigma initiatives, a policy that I highly recommend. Just as Six Sigma will improve your profits, it can also put extra money in your employees' pockets. Six Sigma also compensates in other ways, in the form of higher job satisfaction and personal fulfillment. And these go a long way toward increasing employee dedication and effort, further benefiting the organization as a whole.

Finally, Six Sigma promotes professional development. It gives employees the tools and techniques to think more critically, making them better, more effective employees. Of course this is great for your business, but it's also good for them: it makes them outstanding job candidates to prospective employers.

Let's recap how Six Sigma will affect the people in your organization. A Six Sigma initiative …

- Motivates
  - It involves employees in the real business issues.
  - People are motivated when they have a meaningful purpose.
- Empowers
  - People want to have the skills to fix real-world problems.
  - Fixing a real business problem is liberating!
- Energizes
  - Employees who are allowed to fix costly problems are going to be relentless and loyal to the business.
  - When employees know that their work has greater meaning, they feel invigorated.
- Compensates
  - Contrary to popular belief, employees want more than money. Of course they want money, but they also want to like their jobs, fix real problems, and help the business to fulfill its mission. That's a free compensation system that pays off in loyalty, honesty, and a relentless pursuit of excellence.
- Educates
  - It is an investment in problem-solving skills for your business and in a specific set of tools used to resolve problems. Those skills will benefit employees and owners for decades of improvements. The return on a decade of problem solving is beyond calculation. Go back five or ten years and think about the difference it would have made to rid your company of just 25 percent of the costly defects it has experienced.

> Today, the best-in-class companies provide a tremendous amount of training and education for their employees—and are discovering the rewards. For example, Motorola has realized a 10-to-1 return on its training budget. In fact, it requires every employee to receive 40 hours or more of training annually, of which 40 percent must be in the area of quality. While the same level of investment may be impossible for smaller businesses, the take-away is that the more you can do, the better. It really is an investment in your future.

You can see how Six Sigma positively affects overall employee attitude. In fact, it changes a company's entire way of thinking. I like to call this "injecting Six Sigma into the corporate genetic code," just as Jack Welch said at GE, "Six Sigma is quickly becoming part of the genetic code of our future leadership."

Six Sigma and Company Culture

We hear and read a lot about *corporate culture*, but the term is not limited to large companies. Your business has its own unique culture as well, and it permeates every aspect of your business.

In order to achieve a high level of quality, to reach six sigma, a company must be prepared to change its culture. Just like the CEOs and other top executives of large corporations, owners and managers of small businesses must be prepared to take a serious look at "how things are done around here" and be willing to change. As I have said before, Six Sigma affects the whole organization, including behaviors and attitudes. This necessarily encompasses how people think about various aspects of the company and their beliefs about how it should operate.

> **Corporate culture** The beliefs, values, expectations, behaviors, and ways of operating that characterize the interactions of the people in a business organization.

Six Sigma will bring about a transition from current cultural traits and attributes to a new way of life, beginning with a totally new set of values and perspectives. What do I mean? Take a look at the Figure 2-2.

What are your company's attitudes and beliefs? Does the "Current State" column describe your business? Are you ready to transform your current culture into a Six Sigma culture?

The Role of the Small Business Owner/Manager

Six Sigma will improve every aspect of your business: processes, products and services, customer satisfaction, employee commitment and perform-

Cultural Traits and Attributes	Current State	Future (Six Sigma) State
Outlook	Short term (month to month)	Long term (years)
Focus	Product	Process
People	Seen as a cost	Seen as an asset
Analysis	Experience-based	Statistically-based
Training	Luxury	Investment
Quality	Cost	Return on investment
Behavior	Reactive	Proactive
Problems	Fixing required problems	Preventing with root solutions
Direction	Seat of pants	Measurement, facts, and metrics
Chain of command	Hierarchy	Empowered teams

Figure 2-2. Corporate culture, current and with Six Sigma

ance, company culture, and, of course, the bottom line. But you won't realize any of these benefits if *you* aren't completely dedicated. Are you fully committed? Let's take a moment to consider what is required of you, the owner or manager.

Commitment

First and foremost, you must be firmly committed to implementing Six Sigma. This will require you to dedicate significant time, energy, and company resources. Six Sigma starts with you—and you must lead by example. If you demonstrate clear and unwavering dedication to Six Sigma, your employees will follow!

Leadership

Be prepared to get highly involved from the start and then stay that way. It will be your responsibility to own and drive the Six Sigma journey to quality improvement. Just as you lead your company from day to day, you will be required to lead the Six Sigma initiative. By providing compelling leadership, you will set an example for everyone in the organization to follow. It will be up to you to mobilize your people and to identify the best leaders, organizers, problem solvers, communicators, coaches, and teachers. You must be prepared to think outside the box and you must encourage your employees to do the same.

Encouragement

It will be up to you to encourage the development of a quality environment. The best way to do this is to develop a new *personal vision* for the company, one that promotes a long-term focus on excellence, and then communicate that vision to your employees. And you must encourage and support their active participation.

Promotion

As leader, you will promote the Six Sigma methodology throughout the business. You will be responsible for introducing the entire Six Sigma concept and strategy to your employees, empowering them and supporting their efforts, and embracing and promoting change.

Progress Assessment

Are you ready to begin the Six Sigma journey? Do you have an idea how to get started? Start the following worksheet and see how far you can get. You may not be able to answer more than two or three questions now, but you should be able to answer all of them by the time you finish this book. Do your best—and remember that not knowing is the first step toward understanding!

A Six Sigma Progress Checklist

If you agree with the following statements and can answer the questions, you may already be on the Six Sigma journey.

1. "Customers have critical-to-business expectations."

   Can you list your customers' top four expectations?

   1._____   3. _____

   2._____   4. _____

2. "We are in business to achieve a phenomenal customer satisfaction rate that exceeds critical-to-business expectations."

   Can you quantify your customers' current level of satisfaction? (Y/N)

   If Y, on a scale of 1 to 10, what is it? _____

   How has that changed over the last five years? _____ %

3. "We strive to produce profitable *bottom-line results*. We are in business to make money!"

   List the profits your company has made in the last five years.

   Year 1: $_____

   Year 2: $_____

   Year 3: $_____

   Year 4: $_____

   Year 5: $_____

4. "We have repetitive processes in our business that create products and services for our customers."

   List four major repetitive processes in your business.

   Process 1: _____

   Process 2: _____

   Process 3: _____

   Process 4: _____

   How many times do you do these processes per year? _____

5. "In our process the goal is to create knowledge and actions to reduce cycle time, defects, and variations."

   Take processes 1 and 2 above and list the reduction of cycle time, defects, and variation in those processes.

	Cycle Time	Defects or Yield
Process 1		
Baseline:	_____	_____
Currently:	_____	_____
Process 2		
Baseline:	_____	_____
Currently:	_____	_____

6. "We create knowledge and actions to reduce cycle time, defects, and variations by collecting data, stating the problem in statistical terms such as the mean and standard deviation of the process."

   Does your company know the vital statistics of processes 1-4? (Y/N)

7. "We validate the data collected."

   Is your data validated? Can it be trusted? (Y/N)

   Can you test the data for repeatability and reproducibility by others? (Y/N)

   Is the data accurate and precise? (Y/N)

   If yes, then what are the results of the test?

   _____ percent repeatable and reproducible

8. "We then look for the vital few factors that are the root of the problem by analyzing the data to uncover the vital few factors that determine quality."

   For process 1, what are the vital few?

   Factor 1: _____

   Factor 2: _____

   Factor 3: _____

9. "This moves us into the Improvement phase to create a predictable equation or relationship between the process variables (vital few) and output of the product with a low defect level."

   Can you calculate a result equation—$Y = f(X)$—for process 1?

   What is $Y = f(X)$? _____

10. "We control and sustain the reduction in defects while always quantifying our bottom-line result."

    If process 1 is in the control phase, what are the controls?

    What is the financial result of the project? $_____

11. "We share our knowledge to ensure that everyone understands and benefits from that knowledge."

    How does your company transfer knowledge?

    How quickly is knowledge transferred?

    Is there an infrastructure in place? (e.g., intranet or database sharing)

12. "We as a company achieve our goals, which results in sustained and satisfied internal and external customers."

    What are the goals that you have met in the last two years?

    Goal 1: _____

    Goal 2: _____

Summary

Defects are everywhere! Six Sigma will enable you to eliminate those defects and realize significant cost savings and measurable quality improvement. A small business can't afford to continue operating according to the status quo—those defects could lead to extinction. An extension of TQM, Six Sigma is a precise and *surgical* approach to quality improvement that will generate bottom-line results.

Launching a Six Sigma implementation will require dedication from every member of your organization. It will energize and empower your employees and will affect every aspect of your business. In fact, it will forever change your business culture, forcing you to think outside your company's comfort zone and recognize that there is a better, more efficient way to operate. It is up to you to lead the way! You will need a set of tools to get started and a detailed understanding of the steps you will take on your Six Sigma journey. Let's get going!

Chapter 3

Defining Key Business Metrics for Six Sigma

When you can measure what you are speaking about and express it in numbers, you know something about it, but when you cannot express it in numbers, your knowledge is of a meager and unsatisfactory kind: it may be the beginning of knowledge, but you have scarcely, in your thoughts, advanced to the stage of science.

—Lord Kelvin, British physicist, 1891

avid F. Payton left a 20-year career in healthcare to open a mortgage loan company. When interest rates began to rise, David found himself at a crossroads. How could he make his mortgage business more competitive? In addition to his healthcare background, he was also trained in Six Sigma and he recognized the value of applying Six Sigma to the mortgage industry.

"The defining moment was in my approach to this industry compared with my competitors," said David. "The Six Sigma metric system was my competitive advantage. The credit for my success goes to Six Sigma!"

David understood the value of implementing Six Sigma to streamline processes and reduce cycle times. He saved a lot in operating costs, which gave his company a competitive edge.

The mortgage industry is riddled with variation, unfulfilled promises, low customer satisfaction, and questionable ethics. But David was a process expert and truly understood what it would take to make his business more competitive: make the customer successful. In other words, he recognized that increasing customer satisfaction was the key to his business success. A good system for setting business metrics should begin with *customer* success factors.

Throughout this chapter, I will refer to David and his business to illustrate the importance of your business metrics and to explain the basic concepts behind some of these metrics.

At this point, you have a good feel for how Six Sigma can improve your business. You understand the fundamental concepts, know the benefits, and appreciate the level of commitment required. The first step in planning your own deployment is establishing the business metrics you'll use to gauge results. As stressed in Chapter 1, above all Six Sigma is a data-driven discipline. The use of data starts here—identifying what overall metrics you want to see improve as a result of your Six Sigma investment—and will continue as you work through specific projects and gather data to pinpoint the root causes of problems.

> **Business metric** A unit of measurement that provides a way to objectively quantify performance (of the business as a whole, a unit, a process, etc.). It provides data to help you gauge results and identify areas for improvement.

If you can't measure the quality of something, you won't be able to establish a basis for improvement. In other words, if you don't know where you are, you don't know where you're going. Also, if you can't measure quality, you won't be able to assess the results of your improvement efforts. Think about it—how can you improve quality if you can't measure it?

Examples of Business and Process Metrics

What do you measure in your business? You probably use a number of metrics, which may include some of the following:

- Inventory levels
- Aging of inventory

- Profits and losses

- Cost of goods or services sold

- Return on investment

As you get more and more into Six Sigma, you'll need to supplement these overall business metrics with metrics related to the performance of the processes you're trying to improve, such as:

- **Cycle time** (an important indicator of process *speed*, which is often a key competitive factor)

- **Percent of final products or services with defects** or the number of defects per product or service

- **Hours required** to produce a certain number of outputs or provide a service

- **Customer satisfaction** (extent to which products or services meet customer expectations)

- **Yield** (amount of acceptable goods or services relative to the total number produced or delivered)

- **Cost of poor quality** (a concept we'll cover in a later chapter)

If you haven't set any metrics, I'm surprised you're still in business! How have you made important business decisions without data? Have you relied on your intuition? Have you just guessed?

Imagine for a moment that you're a surgeon. You are in the operating room, about to operate on a man who is suffering from abdominal pain. But you haven't run any diagnostic tests, you haven't asked the patient any questions, and you don't have his previous health records. What do you do? Do you take a wild guess that he has appendicitis and just start cutting? Of course not!

> A recent business survey showed that 89 percent of small businesses that grew reliably for more than three years had in place well-developed methods of tracking their business goals related to growth, incomes, expenses, etc.

Just as a physician uses information to diagnose an illness before beginning treatment, Six Sigma uses metrics to help you identify areas (processes) for improvement. I cannot emphasize to you enough that, as a small business owner or manager, it is absolutely imperative that you track the progress of your company!

The Benefits of Developing Metrics

Developing business metrics and measuring results against them offers several benefits. For one thing, metrics will help you to outline a clear business path for your company. In every business, circumstances change; it's tempting to react impulsively or emotionally. With your numbers in black and white, however, you can make a more rational, informed decision on how to proceed.

Here are some examples of situations that may develop suddenly. Imagine how having solid metrics in place could help determine how to react to these events:

- A competitor cuts its prices.
- New technology changes the way you offer your service.
- Government regulations change and your main product is not in compliance.

To put it simply, companies that pay attention to metrics are able to spot problems and opportunities first. Monitoring and acting appropriately to changes in business metrics are the key to the consistent growth and success of your business.

But how do you know what to measure? Let's look at the criteria for selecting your business metrics.

Good vs. Bad Metrics

Your first instinct at this point may be to measure everything. Don't.

Measuring just to measure is a waste of your time and is not part of the surgical approach of Six Sigma. Rather, you need to choose those metrics that will best help you manage your Six Sigma efforts for the biggest benefit of the company.

Some metrics are good and some are bad. How can you tell the difference? Consider the following:

Good metrics ...

- **Are linked to key criteria:** Measure only those regular processes and activities that will give you relevant information. Never lose sight of your goal: to eliminate waste and defects, fix your processes, and cut costs.

- **Are easy to understand and explain to others:** They should clearly communicate the information you need and should be easy to use. Use units that everyone can understand.

- **Generate feedback quickly:** You need to know how you're doing now. If you're using a metric that comes a month after the fact, you'll always be managing the past, not your current performance.

Bad metrics are the exact opposite! They tell you about things that have no bearing on your business's performance, are complicated, and/or take a long time to generate.

Obviously, your choice of business metrics is key to your success. Your metrics should be key indicators aligned with your company's performance goals. To put it simply, they should be part of what is called your *dashboard*. This term has been used at General Electric for years, by comparison to the dashboard of a vehicle. Picture yourself driving your car. How do you know how fast you are going, how much fuel you have left, or how well the engine is functioning? You look at the gauges on the dashboard to monitor your status. And just as you use the gauges when driving, you use your business metrics to assess your company's current position, check its progress, and identify potential problems.

Determining Relevant Business Metrics

Which business metrics are most relevant to your situation will depend on the answers to two questions:

1. What is vital to the success of your business?

2. What do you want to improve? What are your business goals?

Let's address these questions together, since the answers are the reasons you're reading this book. At a broad level, most issues "vital to success" are subsets of either customer satisfaction (improving quality, features, speed, service) or cost reduction. You need to define these specifically for your own business and use those definitions as the criteria for evaluating metrics. For example, if "cutting delivery speed in half" is vital to your future success, then the most important metrics would be those related to speed. If your overhead costs are too high, then metrics related to inventory or staff levels would be critical. Once you're clear about the criteria, you need to ask more questions.

Fine-Tuning the List of Outcome Metrics for Six Sigma

When deciding which business metrics to track, you must consider the function of each metric and how each is connected to your key criteria. Remember: Six Sigma is about making improvements and connecting them to financial results. Ask yourself the following questions as you establish your metrics:

- What are our business metrics?
- What are the measurement criteria?
- How are the metrics linked to the criteria?
- Do the metrics correlate to competitive advantage?
- If there is no correlation, what does that say about the metrics and criteria we're using? What should we be tracking instead?

If you can answer these questions, then you are defining your metrics correctly.

General Guidelines for Setting and Using Metrics

How do you put your metrics in place and get the information you need? Here are some simple guidelines to follow to get the best results.

Be involved! As owner or manager, you are responsible for setting company strategy, so you and the senior members of your organization must be actively involved in selecting your business metrics. You must make sure that the metrics you choose are directly linked to achieving that strategy.

Display your metrics. Make them accessible and visible to everyone. Use posters, charts, diagrams, etc., so that everyone understands the company's goals.

Limit the number of metrics. As noted above, don't measure everything! It's a good rule of thumb to set no more than five to ten metrics at a time. Otherwise, you may waste valuable time. Also, it's hard to keep track of more than ten.

Act on what you learn. One purpose of these metrics is simply to keep you informed about the state of your business. But equally important is that they should trigger action if you detect problems (e.g., anticipated progress fails to happen). Taking action means you will realize the financial benefits of Six Sigma as soon as possible.

One additional point: be sure your door is open to the questions and concerns of your employees and encourage them to come to you with any problems they encounter with the metrics you've chosen.

Using Metrics to Manage

Once you establish your business metrics, what do you do next?

The first data you collect will establish a *baseline* performance for the business, unit, or process. This is the level against which you'll compare all future performance so you can answer questions such as "Have we improved?" and "By how much?"

> **Baseline** A standard for comparisons, a reference for measuring progress in improving a process, usually to differentiate between a current state and a future state.

Having a firm grasp on where you are now also lets you establish realistic goals for the future, where you want to be by when. There are many ways to set the goal. One is *benchmarking*, doing research within and beyond your company to identify the best-possible performance level out there now. Then you compare your current level and the best-possible level to quantify the goal you want to close.

Another way to quantify goals is to simply crunch the numbers to see what performance level you have to achieve to be competitive. For example, if you know that inventory costs of a certain dollar level are tied to products that are not priced competitively, the market will tell you how much you have to reduce inventory costs to achieve a competitive price.

A third way to establish goals is to use process data to compare current process performance against what's acceptable to customers. This is called establishing *process capability*.

> **Benchmarking** Comparing a process, product, or service against the "best in class" so you can gauge what's possible and identify ways to improve your business.

To quantify goals and measure performance, we use numbers. To better understand those numbers, we use statistics. So, in the next few pages, I'll explain the essentials as briefly and simply as possible.

A Little Statistics

We start with a concept basic to Six Sigma—sigma. You'll recall that sigma is a term used in statistics for standard deviation, an indication of the degree of variation in a set of measurements or a process. So, now we need to discuss standard deviation and variation.

Variation

Variation is "any quantifiable difference between individual measurements." When you improve a process, you should be reducing variation, so you can meet customer expectations more consistently. But to reduce it, you've got to be able to measure it.

There are several ways to measure variation, each with advantages and disadvantages. We'll discuss these methods by suing them in an example.

Your company produces widgets. There are two assembly lines, A and B. You want to reduce the variation in assembly times, so that the workers who package the widgets can work most efficiently—not waiting when widgets arrive late, not falling behind when widgets start piling up, and not feeling pressured to work so quickly that they make mistakes. To track assembly times, you gather the following data:

Process A: 3.7, 6.5, 3.2, 3.2, 5.7, 7.4, 5.7, 7.7, 4.2, 2.9
Process B: 4.7, 5.3, 4.7, 5.4, 4.7, 4.4, 4.7, 5.8, 4.2, 5.7

We can compare those results from the two processes in several ways, using common statistical concepts. (In reality, we would probably collect more than 10 sample values, but that's enough for this example.)

We can use the *mean*. The means would be 5.02 minutes for line A and 4.96 minutes for line B. Their means are very similar. They don't show which process varies more.

We can also use the *median* (the midpoint in our range of data). It's 4.95 for line A and 4.7 for line B. Again, the two values are close. Again, they don't show which process varies more

We can also use the *mode* (the value that occurs most often). It would be either 3.2 (two times) or 5.7 (two times) for line A and 4.7 (four times) for B. So, we can compare 3.2 and 4.7 or 5.7 and 4.7. Either way, the mode doesn't help us much here.

We don't know much about the variations in our two widget assembly lines at this point. None of the three statistical concepts—mean, median, and mode—helps us compare the two lines. Fortunately, there are two more concepts that we can use: *range* and *standard deviation.*

Range is the spread, the difference between the highest value and the lowest value. The range for line A is 4.8 (7.7 – 2.9) and the range for line B is 1.6 (5.8 – 4.2). The range reveals a big discrepancy between the two lines. The variation in A is much greater than the variation in B.

> **Mean** Average (more specifically called the *arithmetic mean*) of the sum of a series of values divided by the number of values
>
> **Median** Midpoint in a series of values
>
> **Mode** Value that occurs most in a series of values
>
> **Range** Difference between the highest value and the lowest value in a series, the spread between the maximum and the minimum

Although range seems to work here, it's a rough measure, because we're comparing only the extremes of the two processes and not the extent of less extreme variation. Range may seem to be a good way to measure variation, but that's not always the case. Let's consider another assembly line, with the following values.

Process C: 3.2, 6.5, 3.4, 6.4, 6.5, 3.3, 3.7, 6.4, 6.5, 3.5

The range for this set of values is 3.3. By that measure, there's less variation in line C than in line A, with a range of 4.8. However, if we use only our common sense, we would realize that the values for C vary more than for A, although they vary less widely.

So range doesn't work in every situation. We need a more accurate way to measure and represent process variation. What mean and mode and median and range cannot do for us, we can get through standard deviation.

Standard Deviation

Standard deviation measures variation of values from the mean. We use the following formula to calculate standard deviation:

$$\sigma = \sqrt{\frac{\Sigma\,(x - \bar{x})^2}{n}}$$

where Σ = sum of, X = observed values, X (X bar) = arithmetic mean, and n = number of observations. That formula may seem complicated, but it's actually simple to understand if we break it down into steps:

1. Find the mean of the process values.
2. Subtract the mean from each of those values.
3. Square the difference for each value. (This step converts any negative numbers to positive for the equation.)
4. Add all of the squared deviation values.
5. Divide the sum of the squared deviation values by the total number of values.
6. Take the square root of that number.

So, when put all of the values for the three lines into our calculator or software, we get these results:

A: standard deviation = 1.81

B: standard deviation = 0.55

C: standard deviation = 1.61

These figures quantify the variation

Standard deviation Average difference between any value in a series of values and the mean of all the values in that series, used as a measure of the variation in a distribution of values.

in each of the assembly lines. We know that the assembly times vary most for line A, almost as much for line C, and much less for line B. This example uses only 10 values for each process and only three processes. But in reality, when we have more processes and/or more measurements and/or a need for greater precision, we appreciate standard deviation more.

Curves and Straight Lines

Now, let's go visual. We'll plot some output values on a chart. This time we'll measure the variation in an assembly line by clocking the assembly times for 100 widgets. When we plot the resulting data points on a histogram (bar chart) and sketch a profile of the bars, it's likely that the distribution of those points will form a curve that's shaped more or less like a bell.

The shape of the curve will vary—one side can be longer than the other, a side can end abruptly or stretch out farther than the other, and so on. However, in a *normal* curve, with both sides taking roughly the same shape, about 68.2 percent of the data points will be within 1 standard deviation of the mean, about 95.5 percent of the points will be within 2 standard deviations of the mean, and 99.7 percent will be within 3 standard deviations.

With your widget assembly lines, as with any process, the goal is to reduce variation. How much? That depends on the customers, internal or external. In this case, your customers would be the employees who package the widgets.

You first determine how much variation your customers consider acceptable. In our example, the widget packagers tell us they'd be happy if the assembly lines produced a widget every five minutes, but that they'd be satisfied if the assembly time was always within a minute of that ideal time.

You then use those values from your customers to set a *lower specification limit* (LSL) and an *upper specification limit* (USL). These lines mark the upper and lower boundaries within which the process must operate.

For your widget assembly lines, you would set an LSL of 4.0 and an USL of 6.0 on your three plots of data points—around a mean of 5.02

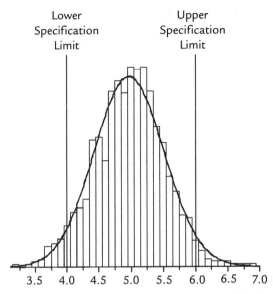

Figure 3-1. Distribution curve and specification limits for line B

minutes for line A, a mean of 4.96 for line B, and a mean of 4.94 for line C. For the sake of simplicity, let's plot only line B (Figure 3-1).

> **Specification limit** One of two values (lower and upper) that form the boundaries for a process between values that are acceptable or tolerated and values that are not.

The standard deviation for line B is 0.55, which is less than the interval between the LSL and the mean (4.96) and the interval between the USL and the mean (1.04). We knew already that the output of line B was within specifications, because none of the 10 times recorded was above 6 minutes or below 4 minutes. However, now we've measured the performance and shown it graphically.

Now, you may be wondering how all of this discussion of variation and standard deviation and curves relates to Six Sigma. It relates because our goal with Six Sigma is to reduce the standard deviation of the variation in a process to the point that six standard deviations (six sigma) can fit within the specification limits.

Through our simple example with widgets, you now know how to use standard deviation to measure the variation in a process and how to graph measurement values to show variation graphically. Next, we move from process *performance* to process *capability*.

Process Capability

Let's switch from manufacturing widgets to selling clothing. A small store has problems with maintaining its inventory level: if they get too low, sales are affected; if they get too high, it ties up too much capital and often causes problems with stocking. The owners decide to set limits for the inventory—a minimum of $11,000 and a maximum of $29,000, Then they track the dollar amounts daily for four months.Look at the Figure 3-2 at how much of the bell-shaped curve is between the two lines labeled as "specification limits."

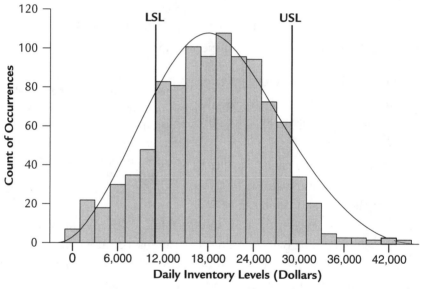

Figure 3-2. Clothing inventory levels daily over four months

As you can see, there's a lot of the curve that is outside the limits. This means that the inventory process is *incapable* of consistently meeting their needs (as defined by the specification limits).

This *degree of fit* between what the process is currently doing and where you need it to be is called *process capability*. The better the fit, the more capable the process. As you can see, it doesn't take a math genius to use data in this way (though having a statistics package on your computer helps). But many companies do like to use process capability as one of their key business metrics and use special statistical calculations to put numbers on the *degree of fit*.

There are two ways in which a process can be *incapable*:

- There may be too much spread or *variation* in the outputs.

Specification limits These are the specifications for outputs of a process. Any output falling within the specification limits is acceptable. Any output falling outside the limits is not acceptable.

Process capability The certainty you have that a process output will meet customer needs (as defined by specification limits).

- The outputs may be off target, centered around an incorrect point.

In terms of improvement, it's important to know which of these conditions is affecting your processes because there are different strategies for correcting the two situations. (We'll get into details in later chapters.)

Using Metrics to Manage a Core Process

Let's go back to David Payton and his mortgage business for a moment and look at how metrics are used to manage a core process.

Though there are no required, industry-wide standards for underwriting, most lenders follow the same basic steps established by government-related agencies, private mortgage insurers, private mortgage investors, or institutional investors:

Step 1. Loan Application

Step 2. Escrow

Step 3. Credit Report

Step 4. Verification

Step 5. Property Appraisal

Step 6. Underwriting/Title Search

Step 7. Interest Rate

Step 8. Closing

Step 9. Customer Service Evaluation (perhaps not a common step, but it should be!)

Nine basic steps, each with a set of sub-steps. David knows from experience that typical process *yield* for each step—the probability of getting through the step without any defects— is 80 percent. The probability of getting through the entire process without any defects is the product of all the steps' yields. This is called the *rolled throughput yield* (RTY) of the process.

> **Process yield** The probability of getting through a step without any defects.
>
> **Rolled throughput yield (RTY)** The probability of getting through an entire process without any defects, calculated as the product of the yields of all the steps in that process.

Here's an example using the nine steps in underwriting a mortgage:

yield 1 x yield 2 x yield 3 x yield 4 x yield 5 x yield 6 x yield 7 x yield 8 x yield 9

80% x 80% x 80% x 80% x 80% x 80% x 80% x 80% x 80% = **13.4%**

In other words, a loan application has a 13.4-percent chance of making it through all nine steps defect-free. David knew that defects were causing rework and reducing the capacity to process a loan efficiently and correctly.

The Cost of Poor Quality

In the mortgage industry, a defect would be any of the following:

- A misspelled name
- An incorrect address
- Transposed digits in a Social Security number
- Missing information
- An erroneous appraisal

You get the idea. Defects such as these can cost a company millions of dollars annually. Consider the cost of a two-month delay on a $100,000 loan at a five-percent interest rate: $833 in lost interest alone, not to mention uncollected service fees and the possibility of losing the consumer to a competitor whose approval process is faster and more efficient. What if David had 50 loans with five-percent delays? That would be a total cost of poor quality of $42,000.

Consider a deposit defect such as a missed zero or a teller forgetting to add the last hour's deposits. How much interest is lost if $5 million is not included in that day's deposits? Many financial institutions have to reconcile their deposits at 1 p.m. to leave time to correct errors. A streamlined, error-free Six Sigma process could allow for reconciliation at 3 p.m., a gain of two hours' worth of interest daily.

The Labor Cost of Defects

Finally, there is the labor cost of defects. It takes a certain amount of time to complete a given transaction. A poor process can compromise cycle times, resulting in major lost labor and opportunity costs. You can use Six Sigma to measure the most efficient cycle time for a given process and to plan and train most effectively. Knowing the demand for services in relation to the day of the week, seasonality, consumer behavior, etc. can also save you substantial amounts of revenue.

So how did David tap into the power of Six Sigma? He began by asking new questions and analyzing the answers:

- What is the average time for one transaction? 15 days
- What is the best performance on a transaction? Five days
- What is the difference between average and best? Ten days
- How many transactions are conducted in a month? 147
- What is the average dollar amount of those transactions per month? $22.3 million

If the best time for a transaction is five days, but the average time is ten days more, that means that one-third of the company's capacity is lost. Multiply that one-third by the average monthly dollar amount to determine the amount of money being lost. And that's only the loan amount; it doesn't include the interest. Do you see a potential Six Sigma project here?

Summary

Before you can begin to apply Six Sigma to your business, you must first ensure that you have metrics in place. Without metrics, it is impossible to improve your processes. You have to establish where you are so that you quantify the gap between that level and where you need to be. And you must *measure* your processes in order to fully understand them.

Process data and other business metrics have a number of uses, including establishing process capability (the likelihood that the process output will meet customer needs) and assessing process yield (the likelihood that any product or service will make it through the process perfectly).

The next step is to gather your resources and begin training. We're getting closer to actually applying Six Sigma to your business.

6σ SB Chapter 4
Staffing Your Six Sigma Initiative

> The greatest achievement of the human spirit is to live up to
> one's opportunities and make the most of one's resources.
> —Luc de Clapiers, Marquis de Vauvenargues

A company president was at a one-day overview of Six Sigma for plant managers and business unit managers. He told them, "You've seen what we're going to do with Six Sigma. I see this happening within the next year. We're going to turn this company around financially. We're going to change everything. I'd like for you to all take part in it, but if you feel you're not going to take part in this effort, let me know right now so we can help you find other employment."

This is an executive with commitment to the vision of doing Six Sigma. There was no question about it. No one thought that Six Sigma was the latest management fad that they could ignore if they liked. He didn't give them a choice. It was "Do Six Sigma or find another place to work."

At this stage, you should have a deeper understanding of your business processes, measuring those processes (i.e., setting your metrics), and linking your metrics to your strategic goals. These are all crucial steps in the Six Sigma journey. Soon you'll be ready to pick your first project and begin applying Six Sigma to your business.

47

But before you can launch your implementation, you will need to consider the resources required to carry it out. These resources include key internal people and their functions, employee training, outside sources of Six Sigma expertise, computer software, and—last but certainly not least—money.

To set the stage, you're probably aware that the big players in Six Sigma implementation have invested an enormous amount of time and money in educating their staff and allocating people to Six Sigma efforts. Typical goals including having ten percent of their staff receive full training and work on Six Sigma projects full-time, with another fourth to half of the staff trained a lesser amount and devoting some fraction of their time to projects. They often demand results in three or four months. Those kinds of numbers sound unrealistic to most small business owners.

However, keep in mind that just because these companies are huge doesn't mean they're casual about how their money is spent. They make these large investments because they know they'll earn them back several times over in business results.

The theme for small business owners has to be to do as much as you can afford to do. The more your people spend on Six Sigma projects and the more you can provide adequate training, the quicker you'll see results and begin to earn that investment back.

On the other hand, the more you relegate Six Sigma to "get to it when you can," the less satisfied you'll be with the initiative. Results will be slow in coming. People will have a hard time tackling larger, more meaningful projects.

That's why the decisions about how much you can afford to invest in training and how many staff you'll devote to project work at what level have to include an evaluation of how important it is that you get results quickly.

With that advice in mind, let's look first at the various players in a typical Six Sigma deployment and then discuss the kind of training these people receive.

Key Six Sigma Players

One reason Six Sigma has been much more successful than its predecessors is because it's not just an improvement methodology. It's also a deployment model. More specifically, Six Sigma prescribes at least five roles that need to be filled and outlines responsibilities for each role:

- **Executive Leaders.** The CEO and top executives, who demonstrate their commitment to Six Sigma and promote it throughout the business.

- **Champions.** High-level executives (people with clout) who design and oversee the deployment effort and who provide ongoing support for everyone involved in projects (making sure resources are available, removing obstacles, etc.). There should be at least one per company. (Some larger corporations have one per unit or division.)

- **Black Belts (BB).** Employees who have completed a basic training course (often four weeks, spread out over a number of months) in Six Sigma methods and tools. They are capable of leading projects and doing a lot of improvement work on their own. Larger companies often target having ten percent of their staff become "certified" Black Belts (meaning they have completed the four-week training and have led a project, the results of which have been verified) and they assign them to work full-time on projects. Smaller companies may have to be satisfied to have only one or a few BBs working part time on projects.

- **Master Black Belt (MBB).** A Black Belt who has received advanced training in one or more specialties within Six Sigma and who has worked on many projects, so he or she has a combination of greater knowledge and more experience to draw from. The MBB acts as trainer, mentor, coach, and guide for the entire organization. Only a small fraction of Black Belts typically become Master Black Belts, so there are fewer even in large companies. Small companies often look to outside resources (an MBB from another company, a private consultant, etc.) to staff this position.

- **Green Belts (GB).** Employees who have completed a shortened training program (often one to two weeks) and have a basic aware-ness of Six Sigma concepts and tools. They are mostly used to staff project teams, working part time on improvement. They rarely lead projects in large companies, but are sometimes required to do so in smaller companies, with some assistance of a Black Belt or Master Black Belt. In large companies, vast numbers of employees receive Green Belt training because the companies see the value in training in basic data analysis and problem solving and they want to have a large pool of people qualified to serve on project teams. Smaller companies can rarely afford to train everyone as Green Belts, but I advise you to do as much as you can.

Some companies include a sixth role, **Yellow Belt,** to denote people who have attended a quick overview of Six Sigma (perhaps two days of training) and who are eligible to serve on teams. (They would need more training to take the lead on any project.)

So you can make better decisions about what level of commitment and training you can afford in your deployment, let's take a closer look at each role and the responsibilities involved.

Executive Leader(s)

That's you! As I wrote in Chapter 2, as the leader of your company, it's your responsibility to introduce Six Sigma, promote it throughout the organization, and engage every single employee's support and participa-tion. It's your job to demonstrate your complete confidence in and com-mitment to Six Sigma—you must show your staff your absolute belief that the Six Sigma initiative will succeed. And, equally as important, you must demonstrate your utmost confidence in your *employees'* ability to succeed. How do you do that? As Executive Leader you will:

- Introduce Six Sigma to the entire organization
- Allocate budgetary funds for training
- Ensure that training happens
- Assign resources

- Use metrics

- Showcase employee achievements

- Recognize key milestones

In other words, as the leader of your business, it will be your responsibility to set things in motion and keep the entire Six Sigma implementation on track and moving forward. By actively demonstrating your commitment, you are promoting and encouraging the development of a Six Sigma culture in your organization. Figure 4-1 shows a model of a memo you might distribute to help get employees on board in your Six Sigma initiative.

If your business doesn't have many employees, however, the personal approach is best. I recommend a kickoff meeting. In order to emphasize the importance of this meeting, if possible, it should be held off-site. If your corporate culture is informal, you might consider holding a dinner meeting at a local restaurant. Only you know what type of meeting will work best for your organization. Regardless of where you decide to hold your kickoff event, make sure to make it memorable.

> **Introducing Your Six Sigma Initiative**
> Depending on the size of your organization, an effective way for you to introduce Six Sigma to your organization is by writing a letter of introduction and distributing a copy to each employee. It should emphasize the importance of Six Sigma and leadership's firm commitment to its success. Here is a sample letter that you can adapt to fit your needs. (See Figure 4-1.)

Champions

Champions, so-called because they support and fight for the entire Six Sigma cause, are essentially the owners of each part of the Six Sigma process. They are absolutely critical to the success of your implementation. They are responsible for the daily oversight and management of every critical element of the Six Sigma initiative. In short, they make it possible for Black Belts to do their jobs. Generally, Champions are drawn from the executive and managerial ranks, but again, it depends on the size of your organization. If you are the only executive in your company, you may have to serve as both Executive Leader and Champion.

From: (President, CEO, or other manager)

To: All Employees

Subject: Six Sigma Implementation

The world today is far more competitive than it has ever been. Customers demand higher quality products, faster delivery, and lower prices, putting great pressure on profit margins across our industry. To survive in this environment, we need to explore new ways to improve our performance. This is the time for us to develop a strategy that will make us the leader in our field.

That strategy is Six Sigma and its improvement methodologies. This strategy will result in substantial cost savings and improved customer satisfaction while increasing profits.

What Six Sigma is all about is incorporating specific methods for eliminating waste and defects in our processes—the ways we go about our business. Six Sigma, successfully implemented, will allow us to take our productivity and profitability to new levels.

You will also be trained in this strategy and its accompanying techniques. Some people will receive more in-depth training and will be directly involved in leading improvement projects that will help us meet our goals.

Six Sigma will require that we make some changes to our culture and the processes by which we get things done. We will all be involved in one way or another in working on improvement projects that will be beneficial to all employees, to the company, and to our customers. I urge you to support and use the tools of this approach to make our company the lowest cost and highest quality provider of goods and services in our industry. As we reach our goals, you will be recognized and rewarded for your participation and support of these efforts.

All our managers are absolutely committed to Six Sigma and have already had training in this methodology. We will be training people at all levels and will begin Six Sigma "Black Belt" training on [date]. Black Belts are designated project leaders who will put together teams and begin Six Sigma improvement projects in various areas. We have selected the [name of company] to assist us in our efforts. Their expertise and guidance will help assure our success.

Your participation, commitment, and support is vital to our success, and we look forward to working with all of you to our mutual benefit.

Figure 4-1. Sample memo announcing Six Sigma to employees

What, specifically, do Champions do? Champions:

- Select Black Belts
- Identify project areas
- Ensure that selected projects are in line with the organization's overall strategy
- Establish clear and measurable goals for projects
- Ensure that the team members clearly understand project goals and links to business strategy
- Keep projects on schedule
- Report to senior management on the progress of projects
- Identify and remove obstacles so that Black Belts can succeed
- Own the results of the Six Sigma implementation

In other words, Champions are in the thick of the Six Sigma battle. To ensure optimal results, they should be fully engaged in the initiative full time.

Black Belts

Black Belts are the heart of Six Sigma. You simply cannot succeed without them. Ideally, Black Belts work full time on selected projects and function as team leaders and project managers. They do the actual work of Six Sigma—they fix the problems, eliminate the defects, and find the money! Black Belts follow the steps of DMAIC (Define, Measure, Analyze, Improve, and Control) to sort through the data, separate opinion from fact, and present in measurable terms the vital few causes of your productivity and profitability problems.

Black Belts:

- Complete a training course (usually four weeks) covering everything from project definition to planning, from basic data analysis to hypothesis testing
- Complete at least one project as part of their training program, with results that are verified several months after completion (i.e., new data is collected to make sure the gains have been sustained)

- Present new ways of doing things
- Challenge conventional wisdom by applying new methodologies successfully
- Pursue project objectives
- Work to understand the causes and effects of defects
- Develop a plan to eliminate the defects permanently
- Ensure that quality improvements are maintained and sustained
- Often lead projects (and therefore must be trained in project leadership skills, such as running effective meetings, working through conflict, etc.)

Throughout the initiative, Black Belts use Six Sigma tools and methods to achieve positive results. Black Belts are your ultimate problem solvers.

In large companies where BBs are allocated full-time to improvement, they are often treated as "roving" experts, assigned anywhere in the company as the need arises (e.g., a BB from finance could end up working in manufacturing or customer service). In smaller companies, where BBs may work part-time on projects, they are usually restricted to work within their functional areas (e.g., a BB from finance would work only on financial projects).

Master Black Belt

Think of a Master Black Belt as a consultant to you, your Champion, and all the other Belts. They have completed their basic Black Belt requirements and training, then gone on to receive additional training and lead many more projects. So they are experts in what it takes to get projects done and produce results.

Master Black Belts perform two roles: they train employees and they act in advisory roles, helping out Black Belts and teams as needed. They need not attend every team meeting. And that's why this is the one Six Sigma role that you can consider having filled by an outsider. What, specifically, does the Master Black Belt do?

The Master Black Belt:

- Conducts Six Sigma training
- Advises on selecting employees for Black Belt and Green Belt roles
- Helps screen and select projects
- Serves as an expert resource, providing the tools and tactics needed to succeed

Once your Six Sigma initiative is well on its way and you've achieved positive results, you can graduate some of your Black Belts to the ranks of Master Black Belts. This will ensure that your initiative stays on track and that you will sustain the results.

Green Belts

In large companies, Green Belts are the "worker bees" of many initiatives, being used to staff project teams. In smaller companies, a Green Belt may be the team leader and the only person on the team with any training. Because their training is more limited and their time for project work is usually limited, they usually work on projects within their own functional area. (Recall that Black Belts often rove among departments.) In other words, they use Six Sigma tools to examine and solve problems on projects within the scope of their jobs.

Green Belt responsibilities usually include:

- Working part time on projects (serving as full team members, even if they aren't leading projects)
- Helping to collect and/or analyze data
- Running experiments
- Conducting tasks important to the project
- Applying their knowledge of the process to problem analysis

As noted earlier, Green Belts usually complete a much shorter training program than Black Belts, but still have a basic understanding of Six Sigma. Their widespread participation helps transform a company culture from the ground up.

Project Team Members

Like Green Belts, Project Team Members work part-time on projects. They represent the various areas that are directly or indirectly involved in the process that is being improved. In other words, Project Team Members should be those employees who work on the process daily, who use the outputs from the process (internal customers), or who provide inputs into the process (internal suppliers).

Key Six Sigma Players in Your Organization

Now that you have a basic understanding of the key players in a Six Sigma initiative, you are probably wondering how these roles will be filled within your organization. What if you have fewer than ten people on your entire team? Figure 4-2 will help you understand how you can apply your people to a Six Sigma implementation.

Regardless of the role played by each participant, he or she must be fully responsible for his or her area. In other words, each employee must be accountable, trustworthy, and dependable. Most important, these key operational roles must be clearly defined *before* you begin your Six Sigma implementation. Every single participant must understand exactly what is expected of him or her and how all of their roles work together on the Six Sigma team.

Now let's discuss how to identify the best candidates for these roles.

Filling Key Roles

What are the criteria for selecting the right people for these key roles? Let's look at each one individually:

Selecting Your Champion

The role of the Champion cannot be overemphasized. This person must be able to understand the strategy, tools, and discipline of Six Sigma and is responsible for selecting projects and Black Belts. He or she will be

Annual Revenue	$1-3 million	$3-7 million	$7-20 million	>$20 million
Employees	<10	10-50	51-100	>100
Champion	Key Supervisor/Manager or President/Owner	President/Owner	Top of org chart	Top of org chart
Master Black Belt	Outside expert or employee with a lot of Six Sigma experience	Outside expert or employee with a lot of Six Sigma experience	Preferably at least one—first to complete BB training, lead initial projects and perhaps receive additional training	One or more (depending on the number of projects)
Black Belt, (100% of time if possible; at least 50%)	1	2-3	5-7	10
Green Belt	1 @ 20% time	1-5 @ 20% time	5-20 @ 30% time	Ideally up to 25% of employees if possible (25 or more) at 30%
Project Team Members	Use customers and suppliers if possible; involve other employees if possible	Six-member project team	Six-member Black Belt project team	

Figure 4-2. Key Six Sigma players and their roles

involved in the Six Sigma efforts every single day. Most important, the Champion will provide the leadership required to keep things on track from day to day. In very small companies, you as the president or owner may need to fill this role. Otherwise, the best person for this role is probably your key supervisor or manager—your right-hand person who is most familiar with the overall operations of your organization.

Selecting Black Belts

Getting results from your Six Sigma projects is critical to getting returns on your investment. The best way to get results is to make sure that the Black Belts leading the projects are dynamic team leaders. While training at the Yellow Belt and Green Belt level is usually open to anyone, Black Belt training is usually offered only to candidates who have made it through a screening process.

The main skill required of a Black Belt is the ability to solve problems. Additionally, he or she should be an outstanding communicator, able to effectively transfer Six Sigma knowledge to others in the organization. It is helpful to be technically oriented, but it is not required. A Black Belt must also have the will to succeed and be able to shoulder the immense responsibilities that come with this role. With that in mind, your Champion should use the following selection tool (Figure 4-3) to identify the best candidate for the role of Black Belt. In filling this out, use the following scale:

5 = excellent

4 = above average

3 = average

2 = below average

1 = unacceptable

Scoring: Above 38 is an excellent Black Belt candidate.

Selecting Green Belts

Green Belt training should be available to as many employees as you can afford to train. The basic skills they learn are useful not just for project work but also in improving their jobs. Use the same selection tool (Figure 4-3) to identify the best employees to train as Green Belts. In this case, a score of 35 or better indicates an excellent Green Belt candidate

Assembling a Project Team

The option that most small businesses use for assembling project teams is very simple: accept anyone who volunteers! The team leader should be an

Attribute	Score
Process and product knowledge	
Basic statistical knowledge	
Knows the organization	
Communication skills	
Self-starter, motivated	
Open-minded	
Eager to learn new ideas	
Desire to drive change	
Team player	
Respected by others	
Track record on results	
Total Score	

Figure 4-3. Rating a Black Belt candidate

employee who has received or is receiving formal Six Sigma training, ideally a Black Belt (or trainee), but many companies use Green Belts.

The size of the team will vary greatly by company and by need. At one end of the scale, for a very limited project, you could assign a Black Belt candidate and one other employee. The ideal team size is about five to seven people: that's enough to represent a wide range of views but not so large as to be cumbersome. Forming that team would be a Black Belt

Involve Customers and Suppliers

Whenever the process you're targeting touches the outside—i.e., uses inputs from outside suppliers or delivers a product or service to external customers—it's a good idea to include representatives from those groups on your teams. That gives you a chance to hear about their needs and challenges directly.

If you don't put customers or suppliers on your teams, at least gather data directly from them. Ask your customers to participate in surveys designed to improve the process and ask them questions. Do the same with your suppliers. These "outsiders" are integral to your processes.

or a Green Belt, team members drawn from the affected work area, and perhaps a customer or a supplier.

Training and Training Resources

Training is vital to Six Sigma. Without it, your implementation will not succeed. As you may have noticed above, what distinguishes the various levels of Belts is not the time they work on projects or their roles on project teams but rather the amount of training and experience they have (as summarized in the sidebar).

Training Requirements

Black Belt: four weeks of training on all phases of DMAIC, data collection and analysis, effective teamwork, and project management *plus* completion of one project

Master Black Belt: basic Black Belt training *plus* additional training on expert topics (such as lean manufacturing, design of experiments, Design for Six Sigma)

Green Belt: an abbreviated Black Belt course (often just one week) that covers the highlights

Yellow Belt: a one- to two-day overview course

Executive Leader, Champion: minimally, a two-day overview course on the basic concepts of Six Sigma and making strategic decisions about where, when, and how to deploy Six Sigma; ideally, additional training (more like Green Belt or Black Belt training) for the Champion

---

Getting enough training for Black Belts and Master Black Belts used to be a big challenge for small businesses. But that is no longer the case. Six Sigma training is now available all over the world from a wide variety of sources.

How do you obtain the training that is so vital to Six Sigma success? We can steal the approach of Graham Richard, the mayor of Fort Wayne, Indiana, who trained dozens of city employees at a fraction of the price that large corporations pay. He calls it the *four B's*:

- **Beg:** Ask if you can piggyback your training with courses being offered in large companies locally. If you are a supplier to large companies, one or more may have an active Six Sigma program (or something very similar) and may let you send one or two people to their training. There may also be quality networks in your area that would let a few of your staff attend training at discounted prices.

- **Borrow:** It's unlikely that another company would lend you a Black Belt, but companies may have internal experts (Master Black Belts) who could spend several hours a month helping you plan your deployment and train your staff.

- **Buy:** If the first two options don't work, look around for packaged training programs that you could purchase or send your staff to, perhaps through a local technical college or quality network. You can also hire an external consultant (sometimes called an *implementation partner*) to develop and deliver training to your staff. See below for more details on these options.

- **Build:** If all else fails, the last resort is to build your own training program from scratch. This can be very time-consuming and, if not done by people who are knowledgeable in Six Sigma, it won't serve your purposes, so you'd be better off going with one of the first three options!

Working with an Implementation Partner

I would estimate that there are approximately 200 consultants in the field of Six Sigma worldwide. The best way to find them is via the internet. Google "Six Sigma consultant" and you will get thousands of hits. A reputable consultant will help you to orchestrate all responsibilities, roles, and schedules to make a smooth transition from planning to implementation. He or she will function as your Six Sigma expert (Master Black Belt) and should provide all the necessary training and materials to ensure that your Six Sigma deployment is a success.

Unfortunately, it is my opinion that there are very few implementation partners out there that offer what I term the *Real Six Sigma*.™ And of course, hiring an outside consultant can cost a significant amount of money—that you may or may not be willing or able to invest.

If you decide to consult an outside expert, you will need to ensure that the consultant is qualified. How do you determine if a consultant is "the real deal"? I offer the following advice for evaluating potential imple-mentation partners.

First, check credentials! Be diligent and sort fiction from fact. There are an awful lot of people and organizations purporting to be Six Sigma experts. You should request references and case studies from bona fide clients. In other words, you want proof of results. After all, that's what Six Sigma is all about.

Examine how the consultants structure their fees. Do they require payment on the basis of their billable hours or do you pay them only when you see results? In other words, are they willing to share the risk with you by getting paid based on their performance? In theory, either type of consultant should be committed to your success regardless of how they get compensated, but I would be more likely to trust the consultant who is working toward the same objective as you: financial results.

But how do you know if you are getting your money's worth? How do you know that you are really getting real Six Sigma expertise? I recom-mend that you use my Six Sigma Scorecard (Figure 4-4) to ensure that your implementation partner delivers the Real Six Sigma. If a consultant can pass this test, you are on the right track to Six Sigma success.

Educational Resources

Of course there are other sources of Six Sigma training that do not require you to bring an outside expert into your organization: community colleges and universities. There are two directions you can take when choosing the academic route: on-campus courses and distance or online learning.

On-Campus Training Courses

Many schools offer continuing education training for Green Belts and Black Belts. Contact the Continuing Education or Executive Education departments to inquire about their programs. Some also provide cus-tomized training for local businesses: they will create a training program for your organization, with your specific needs in mind. Tuition costs and hours required for completion vary. Most of these courses are not offered for college credit toward a degree, but students should receive CEUs (con-

Six Sigma Key Success Elements	Training Partner	Check
CEO Commitment	Requirement	✔
Executive Training	2-3 day working session with pre-work prerequisite with specific deliverables along with certification requirements	✔
Select Brightest and Best	Pre-screening requirement, tools on selection, CEO memo to reinforce	✔
Financial Benefit	Guaranteed 4 times in **writing**	✔
Black Belt Training Method	Standard topic, sequence, content, instructor notes included	✔
Time and Dedication by Black Belt	Requirement	✔
Executive Reward System	Requirement	✔
Number of Projects Completed per Year	Average = 5	✔
Financial Validation	Requirement before, during, and after	✔
Six Sigma a Priority	Requirement for top level priority	✔
Results COPQ % of Revenue $	10%–20% over 3 years	✔
Average Project Time to Complete	4-6 weeks after training	✔
Project Back Log or in Pipeline (Project Inventory)	Required to have 3-5 projects per Black Belt	✔

Figure 4-4. The Six Sigma scorecard

tinuing education units, i.e., credits) from an accredited institution, as well as Green Belt or Black Belt certification. Certification carries real clout in the business community: anyone with certification has completed all required training and has the full capability of a Green Belt or Black Belt. A good program will require a Green Belt candidate to complete one Six Sigma project and should require a Black Belt candidate to complete two Six Sigma projects. An implementation partner should offer certification for your Green Belts and Black Belts.

Distance/Online Learning

Distance learning, also known as "e-learning," has exploded in recent years. Most educational institutions now offer it. Not surprisingly, there are countless Six Sigma e-learning Green Belt and Black Belt courses, offered by community colleges, universities, and Six Sigma consulting organizations. Again, the internet is your best means of finding the right source.

The advantages of obtaining certification through e-learning are obvious: employees can take the courses according to their time schedules, classroom attendance is not required, and the courses are often less expensive than traditional courses. Be careful, however, to choose an accredited institution with a solid academic reputation or a consultant whose credentials you have verified. As always, make sure that you are getting the best possible training for your money.

Computer Software

The purpose of this book is to simplify Six Sigma and make it possible for you, the small business owner/manager, to do it on your own. But there are also software programs on the market designed to make your implementation easier; they can save you significant time and aggravation. In effect, these programs are part of the Six Sigma toolset. I recommend visiting www.isixsigma.com for research on tools for Six Sigma.

Most Six Sigma software is designed for *support*. In other words, most programs are made to supplement the materials you already have and they require a certain level of Six Sigma knowledge in order to use them effectively. Minitab and SigmaFlow are two of the vital few programs that will help you with your implementation.

These software programs can be expensive if you buy them at retail outlets, but you can find them on the internet at substantial discounts. eBay, for example, sells many used or even new versions of these programs. You may also be able to obtain them at a student discount from the community college or university where you receive your Six Sigma training.

Additional Resources: Time and Money

Obviously, training your employees will take time, which may cause you some concern. But throughout this book I have emphasized over and over again that your absolute commitment to your Six Sigma deployment is vital to eventual success. That commitment obviously involves time. Yes, it will take time to train your people—but it will be well worth the time and effort expended!

There is one last resource that I have neglected to mention until now: money. Don't get me wrong: I know that cost is a substantial concern for small business owners. In fact, money is an obstacle for many businesses, regardless of size. And it is true that undertaking a Six Sigma initiative will cost you some money. Only you can determine how much money your organization is willing and able to spend. There are so many options for training out there that you should not have any trouble finding a program that fits your needs and your budget.

You may also be concerned about taking employees away from their regular jobs to function as Black Belts. But one of the main goals of Six Sigma is to increase your profits: by applying Six Sigma to your business, you will achieve real, measurable financial results. So, ask yourself the real question: "How can I afford *not* to do Six Sigma?"

Moving Forward—Plan It!

Let's assume at this point that you have identified candidates to fill the roles of Champion, Black Belt, Green Belts, and Project Team Members. Let's also assume that you have selected a training source and you are ready to go.

Before you jump right in, you need to know how to plan for your Six Sigma implementation. A well-executed plan of action will get you off to the best possible start on your journey to Six Sigma success.

Advance Planning Required to Launch Your Six Sigma Initiative

There are certain phases in Six Sigma planning that serve as the foundation for an implementation and certain steps to take.

Step One: Communication and Education

Introduce Six Sigma. As I stated earlier in this chapter, the first step in your Six Sigma journey is to introduce Six Sigma to the entire organization. This should be done via a letter from you, the Executive Leader, or at a kickoff event off-site. This will set the tone for the entire deployment and clearly demonstrate your commitment.

Educate Yourself. The more you know about Six Sigma and what it can and cannot accomplish, and what it takes to make results happen, the better you'll be able to plan and oversee your initiative. Reading this book is a good start, but you'd be even better off if you could attend an executive awareness session (perhaps prevail on a local company to attend their session!). Better still, check around for companies in your area that are doing Six Sigma and arrange to visit them. The practical insights you'll gain— and the opportunity to ask questions of someone already involved in Six Sigma—will be invaluable. (And of course, if you choose to be trained and certified as a Green Belt or a Black Belt, all the better!)

Step Two: Select Your Champion and Black Belt and Green Belt Candidates

Select Your Champion. You probably already know who will perform this function. It could be your partner, your key supervisor or manager, or even you.

Select Black Belt(s). As discussed above, Black Belts are chosen carefully based on criteria shown to be important for project success. Develop a list of potential Black Belt candidates and look closely at each of them. Your Champion should use the selection tool (Figure 4-3) to choose the best candidates to fill the role of Black Belt. Then, create a job description for this new role. Finally, determine how you will reward your Black Belt upon completion of projects.

Select Green Belts and Project Team Members. The best advice I can give here is to ask for volunteers. These employees will likely be expected to put in a lot of extra time on project work—above and beyond their regular work jobs. So you don't want people serving on your project teams who don't want to be there! If you can afford to provide some of these employees with minimal training (at the Green Belt or Yellow Belt level), so much the better.

Step Three: Train Staff

Once you've selected people to fill the key roles, it is time to train them. Decide how and when you will make training happen (remember the four B's: beg, borrow, buy, build). Make sure that you have provided your Green Belt and Black Belt students with all of the information and materials they need to complete their training successfully.

Step Four: Pick the First Project

Here we are, finally: it is time to pick your first project. The goal is to choose a project that will be successful and return maximum results. Selecting your project is the focus of the next chapter.

Summary

At this point you may feel overwhelmed. There is so much to do before you can even begin applying Six Sigma to your business. But all of these steps are absolutely necessary to lay the foundation for a successful implementation; don't skip or eliminate any of them! You must communicate your Six Sigma vision to the entire organization, you must gather your resources, you must select people to fill key roles, you must obtain training, and you must dedicate time and money to this initiative. Once you've taken these important steps, you can move on to the next phase in the Six Sigma process: picking your first project!

6σ
SB

Chapter 5
Selecting Your Six Sigma Project

Money isn't the most important thing in life, but it's reasonably close to oxygen on the "gotta have it" scale.

—Zig Ziglar

Not long ago I was working with a small medical practice to streamline their administrative processes. By chance, I was asked by one of the doctors to join in a discussion about anemia—they wanted to know if there was an application for Six Sigma. It seems that a number of their patients were suffering from this common blood disorder, but the doctors had been unable to determine a definitive cause. Instead, they had simply been treating their patients' symptoms; unfortunately, these patients were experiencing a significant decline in their quality of life. I informed the doctors that this was a problem that Six Sigma could solve rather quickly.

Using the "Y" is equal to the function of "X" formula, we identified possible causes of anemia. Anemia X's included the following:

- Increased breakdown of red blood cells
- Increased blood loss from the body
- Inadequate production of red blood cells

We next pulled a sample data set accounting for 286 active patients. Of those, 23 percent suffered from the type of anemia that is caused by blood loss. Blood loss was the "Y" we needed to solve for these patients. Using Six Sigma tools, we looked for possible X factors driving the blood loss, and found that for 17 percent of them, the root cause was literally going down the toilet. Blood was being passed through the stool of the patients due to massive hemorrhoids! A basic surgical procedure was the solution to the problem, and after many years of poor health, these patients are living full lives again. The cost of the surgery was $7000, compared to an average cost of $78,000 over a two-year span of unnecessary treatments, ER visits, medications, and so on.

This project, which took about one month, saved a lot of money. But ultimately and more importantly, it dramatically improved the patients' (customers') health and quality of life.

Now that we've learned some of the basics of Six Sigma and how it can help you, you're now ready to finally begin *applying* Six Sigma to your small business. Where should you start? We'll begin by picking your first project, the one that will be the most successful and give you maximum results. Project selection is perhaps the most important component of the Six Sigma methodology—pick the wrong project, and you will actually lose money because you could be applying improvement resources to something that won't have much payback

You've probably been thinking about potential projects for a while. I would be willing to bet that you've already identified a few chronic problems you would like to investigate and improve. But there are some important criteria you should consider for choosing Six Sigma projects— selecting the most obvious is not always advisable, and every business scenario is not a potential "project." Let's examine these key criteria.

Key Criteria for Project Selection

First of all, what is the purpose of a Six Sigma project? To identify a specific problem or set of problems and then solve it with your designated Black Belt(s) to capture hidden revenue and increase customer satisfaction. That means that Six Sigma doesn't need to be used in every instance.

For example, let's say that you are consolidating your business, and you need to reduce your facilities from two to one. Is this a Six Sigma project in the making? Should you allocate Six Sigma resources and get your Black Belt(s) on the job? No. You should simply sell the extra building and move its assets into the remaining facility—there is no need to collect data because you already know what should happen! This type of scenario requires a decision and the appropriate action, nothing further. In other words, if the solution is in front of you and you know it, then just do it and don't waste your valuable Six Sigma resources.

Effort and Probability of Success

There are two important criteria for a successful project: the *effort required* and the *probability of success*. What do I mean? First, you must have a good understanding of the duration of the potential project in relation to the return on investment. In other words, it could take more time than the project's duration before you see monetary results. To put it simply, you must evaluate your effort in terms of the resources you deploy (Black Belts, expenses, etc.), and the time it takes until those resources produce for you. In everyday terms, we're talking about doing an informed cost-benefit analysis to determine the best place to deploy your Six Sigma efforts.

Second, you should consider the probability of success for a project. Examine the potential risks of the project, and think about the time, effort, and implementation factors to figure out if a potential project is desirable. Use the matrix shown in Figure 5-1 on the next page to help do this.

The Low-Hanging vs. Rotted Fruit

A good example of finding a gold mine in a process happened when I went to the production site of a potential new client for an assessment visit. The company made a control cable for automobile cruise control systems, which is made of a half dozen or so individual cables. I looked around and saw money all over the floor: four- to six-inch pieces of cable lying there, which had been trimmed because the company's process was not precise enough to get the correct length on the first pass. As I laid these pieces out end-to-end, I asked the plant manager, "What do you

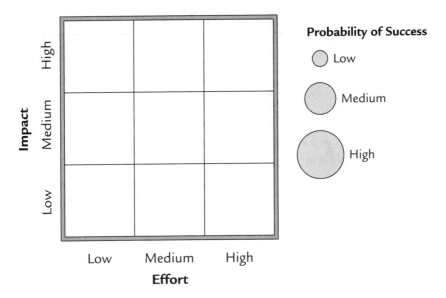

Figure 5-1. Project desirability matrix

see?" He had no answer until the lengths approached the full measure of a final cable, when he finally realized that the waste on the floor represented a whole lot of complete cruise control cables! At six cents per foot, each six-inch wasted piece was worth about three cents. When you add that up over time, it amounts to a considerable waste of money.

If you want to fill your bushel basket as quickly as possible, you pick the low-hanging fruit, right? The same is true of Six Sigma projects. On the other hand, I refer to the type of cost savings represented by the wasted cruise control cable as *rotted fruit*. Your organization's normal quality and cost control systems should address obvious rotted fruit such as this! It's better to choose the *low-hanging fruit*, or the easiest targets that will show results as quickly as possible and will build momentum for your entire Six Sigma implementation.

A good rule of thumb is to select a project that has a low ratio of effort to impact. In other words, its benefit should outweigh the cost and effort required to make it happen.

> Let's emphasize the priority for selection: Choose a project that offers a high-value outcome for limited effort!

Scoping a Project

Another factor to consider when selecting a project is *scope*. The scope of your project should be manageable, but not so narrow that the solution is obvious, as I mentioned earlier. For the purposes of your small business, I recommend that your first project be one that is small and well focused.

> **Project scope** This is the size of the project and the amount of resources required to take it on in relation to the expected results. Early on, the scope of your project should be small so you can use it as a learning experience and give your people a chance to have a quick success.

Keep in mind that it's possible to produce more than one positive result from the same project. If your project affects the three elements of your business that are critical to your customers' expectations (i.e., quality, cost, and delivery), you will maximize the impact of your project.

In addition, scoping your project will allow you to effectively identify the resources that you will need to complete the project, and it will enable you to establish a timeframe for carrying it out.

Project Ideas

Pause for a moment and look back at the readiness assessment you completed at the end of Chapter 2. Do you see any potential Six Sigma projects? What are the problems currently confronting your business? Take a look at customer complaints you have received. Think back to meetings you've had with your staff—what are the problems that come on a daily basis? If you look at those aspects of your business that are most critical to your overall success, you will find a gold mine of potential projects. Consider the following factors.

The Cost of Poor Quality

As I have stated time and again, Six Sigma is about eliminating defects. Defeating your organization's defects means defeating the *cost of poor quality*, or COPQ. COPQ is the criterion by which you judge your potential projects.

> **Cost of Poor Quality (COPQ)**
> The time, materials, and resources expended in nonproductive, non value-added products and services, such as fixing a problem for a customer after the poduct has been delivered. It is also known as "the cost of doing it wrong." If you don't have to expend money on this, you immediately improve your bottom line, not to mention lowering your blood pressure.

Remember that one of the main reasons you're implementing Six Sigma within your organization is to save money. Eliminating defects with a measurable cost attached to them will produce the results you're looking for. So be sure to pick a project that has cost savings attached to it—in other words, don't focus on activities that fail to cut costs!

Examine the COPQ factors for your business. Are there any obvious, quick "fix-its" that were put in place to temporarily fix a problem, i.e., any band-aids that have failed to address the real problem? These "fix-its" are potential projects in the making. Some examples might be:

- Excess inventory
- Rework and repair
- Overstaffing
- Duplicate and excess paperwork
- Expediting
- Inspections
- Replanning

All of these temporary "fix-its" fail to rectify the root cause of a problem in the process, and they are common COPQ factors.

Non-Value-Added Factors

Non-value-added factors are activities that add costs but no value for customers. These activities provide potentially great targets for Six Sigma projects. These non-value-added activities might include the following:

- Downtime
- Material handling
- Sorting and stacking
- Delivery expediting

- System utilization
- Inspection and rework
- Data entry rework
- Requoting

Identifying and determining the causes for any one of these activities and eliminating them by improving the process can be a good Six Sigma project resulting in immediate cost-savings improvements.

Value-Added Factors

Value-added activities can also be sources for Six Sigma projects. These are the activities that are vital to your business, and that directly impact the customer. They include:

- Assembly
- Order entry
- Billing
- Processing transactions
- Fulfillment rate

Selecting one of the processes as a Six Sigma project will improve the service you provide to your customers. Remember, one of the goals of Six Sigma is to improve customer satisfaction!

Take a look at Figure 5-2, which deals with personal living expenses, and you'll see the connection between these factors, Six Sigma projects, and the expected results.

Critical-to-Quality

What are the major issues confronting your business? What factors are critical to your success? Basically, there are three elements associated with any business: sales, profits, and costs. Whether you are working in sales, marketing, manufacturing, or any other arena, each and every one of your processes has a connected cost. Your job is to identify that cost and establish a measurement to assess its effects on your ability to profitably deliver quality products and services to your customers.

The Project Problem Statement

Remember when you were in high school and you were assigned to write a report? How did you begin? If you're like me, it was with a thesis statement that set forth the subject and purpose of your report. The Six Sigma problem statement is similar in that it communicates the purpose of your project and focuses the organization on the process deficiency to be fixed.

To be effective, the statement should be quantifiable and specific; in other words, it presents the numbers that illustrate the problem, and spells out cost and customer satisfaction issues to be addressed.

Here is an example of a good project problem statement:

Currently the MIS application is causing five days in delays affecting four multiuser capabilities, which are adversely costing $2,000 in excess labor per month along with $18,500 in interest cost per year.

On the other hand, here is an example of a bad project problem statement:

We feel that by developing a new MIS application to replace the existing application would result in an increase in productivity, and we believe the employees would be motivated to perform at higher levels. This would cost only a little over $10,000 for installation and only $500 per user seat.

Does this statement make sense? Does is set forth the purpose of the project? It's more wishful thinking than specifics, and this is why it is a poor problem statement.

The Project Objective Statement

Once you've written a good project statement, you should follow with a strong objective statement that communicates how the problem is going to be solved. This should include where you are right now, what needs to be done to change the process, the expected duration of the project, and the expected cost savings.

Here is an example of a poor project objective statement:

We need to increase productivity by installing a new application.

The problem is that it's too general. Here is an example of a well-written project objective statement:

The objective of the project is to reduce the five days of delay to one day and a user capability to unlimited user base with a minimum of 10 users or better.

Do you see the difference? This one gives the specifics.

A Good Project

A good project will improve your bottom line. How? By fulfilling, or even exceeding your customers' expectations of quality, cost, and delivery. The following is a list of characteristics that make a Six Sigma project successful. A good project will:

- Reduce actual spending
- Reduce accounts payable and net inventory and/or increase accounts receivable
- Improve quality and service levels
- Increase sales by unit volume or net price
- Show results in not more than three months
- Not require a major monetary investment to implement project recommendations
- Have historical data on process performance already available (i.e., you've measured it before)
- Focus on a problem that you have not been able to easily solve
- Allow you to achieve your objectives

A successful Six Sigma project also provides a real learning experience. To sum it up, a good project will fit the following SMART criteria:

S – Specific

M – Measurable

A – Achievable

R – Realistic

T – Time-bound

In other words, you know what you're going to do and why. You can measure the problem and the results. It's something you can achieve with the effort available. It's a real problem that you can fix. And you can fix it in a specific time period.

A Bad Project

OK, so what makes a project "bad?" The scary thing is that it's often difficult to distinguish between a good and a bad project until after you've started. Here are the characteristics of a bad project. Keep these in mind as you start the process of picking your first project.

- The effort required is either minimal or excessive
- The overall impact is slight, i.e. it doesn't produce measurable, financial results
- It is unlikely to succeed because it lacks focus, a manageable time frame, or does not have support from organizational leaders

Here are some examples of bad projects:

- Fix an entire operational function
- Fixing a project with no benefit to the business
- Working on processes that are becoming obsolete
- Validating the capability of a process
- Projects with long-term (>3 years) benefits, and no short-term benefits

Using Your Data: Pareto Charts

Remember that the Six Sigma methodology is data driven. Not surprisingly, you can use data to help you pick a project and send it in the right direction.

The Pareto chart was created in 1906 when an Italian economist named Wilfredo Pareto discovered the principle it illustrates. A Pareto chart separates factors and charts them in descending order from most troublesome to the least. It's a tool to identify the "vital few" that can make the biggest difference in solving a problem.

The Pareto Principle states that, in general, 80 percent of trouble comes from 20 percent of the problems. In other words, only 20 percent of problem causes are vital, while the other 80 percent are trivial. How does this apply to project selection? You begin by performing a Pareto analysis, which involves three levels of charting.

We're going to use a personal financial situation to illustrate this. I worked with a friend to help him get his financial problems under control using Pareto analysis as a first step in identifying the source(s) of his problem. I started the process by asking for the family checkbook, and all receipts (including grocery) for the last year.

Monthly Cost Item	Dollars
House	5,155
Car	1,300
Children	1,000
Insurance	160
Entertainment	1,300
Finance	1,025
Other	2,305
Health care	550
Maintenance	550
Total	$13,095

Figure 5-2. Monthly personal expenses

The first-level Pareto analysis shows that most costs came in the catergories of house, car, entertainment, and finance, and other. However, if you look at the cumulative percent (Cum %), 74.2 percent or close to 80 percent of the cost is in house, other, and car.

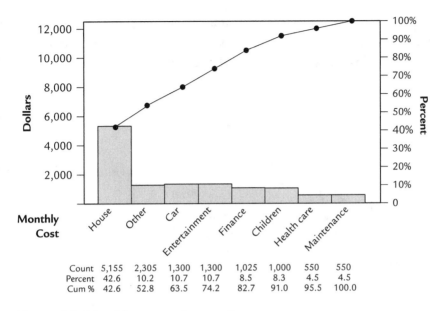

Figure 5-3. Monthly personal expenditures

This was a big surprise to my friend. He asked "So what do we do next?" The next step is to break down these cost items into more detailed categories to see which parts of them are most costly (Figure 5-4).

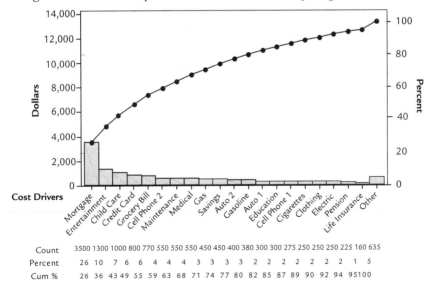

Figure 5-4. An expanded Pareto chart of personal expenditures

My friend's goal was to reduce total monthly expenses by 15 percent. We noticed that 10 percent of the cost was being consumed by "other," so we drilled down to the second level Pareto (Figure 5-5):

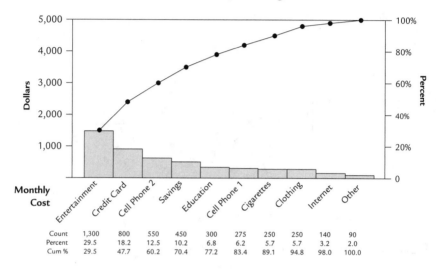

	Entertainment	Credit Card	Cell Phone 2	Savings	Education	Cell Phone 1	Cigarettes	Clothing	Internet	Other
Count	1,300	800	550	450	300	275	250	250	140	90
Percent	29.5	18.2	12.5	10.2	6.8	6.2	5.7	5.7	3.2	2.0
Cum %	29.5	47.7	60.2	70.4	77.2	83.4	89.1	94.8	98.0	100.0

Figure 5-5. Second level Pareto of "other"

We both agreed that 60 percent of the total "other" expenses were mostly waste, and some basic planning could reduce his costs without creating major problems. There was no budget or planning to know what could and could not be spent. There was no checking of the monthly expenses. The "entertainment, credit card, cell phones, and cigarettes were 73.2 percent of the total expenditures. The cell phone detailed billing could have been a third-level Pareto by incoming and outgoing calls by both cells phones. However, the solution would be to renegotiate the billing and limit the minutes of the biggest abuser.

We drilled down to the second level on the house expenses and found a billing error, and other items to pick for projects (Figure 5-6).

There was a utility company billing error because of reading the meter incorrectly, and the focus of that project was to correct the current bill and get a refund for past errors. The result of this was that the utility expenses were reduced from 7.7 percent of the total expenditure to less than 1 percent. The grocery bill became a great project where they created a third level Pareto from the past receipts.

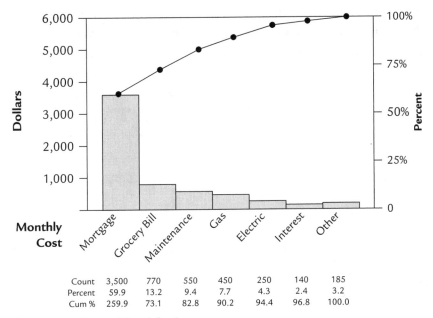

Count	3,500	770	550	450	250	140	185
Percent	59.9	13.2	9.4	7.7	4.3	2.4	3.2
Cum %	259.9	73.1	82.8	90.2	94.4	96.8	100.0

Figure 5-6. Second level for house expenses

In the end, it was apparent that smoking was something my friend could definitely do without. He became a strong advocate of data analysis and worked toward reducing overall expenditures by 23 percent.

You can use this same sort of Pareto analysis to dig down into problems that are most appropriate for a Six Sigma problem-solving project.

Picking Your Project

There is a lot to consider when selecting a Six Sigma project. And I can't emphasize enough that if you fail to pick a good project, you will waste valuable time, resources, and money; and you won't accomplish your Six Sigma goals. Be sure to carefully evaluate each potential project with your Champion and Black Belt—be an active and involved executive leader! Figure 5-7 is a checklist to help you stay focused and on track. If the project you select meets these criteria, it is time to implement the first phase of your Six Sigma implementation: the Define Phase.

Directions: Briefly describe your potential projects at the top of the columns. Evaluate each project using the 17 characteristics listed. (The characteristics are explained on the next page.) If the project satisfies the characteristic, place a check mark in the column. Each project must have at least one of the business impacts listed in items 1-7, and satisfy item 8. Projects having more check marks are preferable to those having less.

Project Description →	Project #1	Project #2	Project #3	Project #4
Characteristics				
1. Increases sales				
2. Increases cash flow				
3. Reduces costs				
4. Avoids costs				
5. Reduces cycle time on bottleneck operation				
6. Increases quality				
7. Increases service				
8. Narrowly focused (achievable in 3 months)				
9. High probability of implementation				
10. Historical data is available				
11. Likely to require little or no capital/ expense investment				
12. Solution is not known				
13. Aligned with your own objectives				
14. Aligned with your manager's objectives				
15. Has failed previous quick fix attempts				
16. Necessary team members are available				
17. Personal knowledge of process				

Figure 5-7. Project selection checklist

Summary

Selecting a Six Sigma project can be a challenging, even daunting task. It takes time and patience to identify those projects that will provide the highest impact for the least amount of effort. But again, taking the time to carefully consider your organization's objectives and your customers' expectations will bring you the greatest results. Make sure that everyone in your organization is involved—remember, Six Sigma is a team effort. We'll now move on to the Define Phase, and begin applying Six Sigma to your business.

| 6σ | Chapter 6 |
| SB | **Your Six Sigma Project: The Define Phase** |

When you confront a problem you begin to solve it.
—Rudy Giuliani

Confronting the problem is defining it!

A small business owner decided to consult with an outside marketing "expert" with the goal of growing the business. Over the next two years, the company's marketing costs increased by $285,000 per year, but sales dropped by 43 percent. Somehow, the company's key customer value-added proposition got lost in the process. The old marketing methods were abandoned while the outside expert effectively took control of the company. In the end, the outside expert produced no result. The company would have been better off not hiring the outside expert and saving the money. What do they do now and for the next year?

The objective for the marketing expert was to grow the company, but this business did not establish measurable goals for the first quarter, let alone the first and second year. What a shame to waste $570,000 without any milestones or accountability for the outside expert! The combination of capital wasted and the distraction of non-value-added activity almost cost this company its life.

In that case, Six Sigma became a problem-solving autopsy that showed the company hadn't confronted the problem, hadn't taken the time to simply define the problem, and hadn't established measurable goals for the first quarter. The owner eventually became aware of the problem, that the growth he wanted was turning into a death spiral for his company. The owner had good intentions—but intentions should never be used to justify actions. You must focus on the problem you are trying to solve.

> **Do Not Worship Gurus!**
> It is OK to get data from the experts or a guru, but you must get corroborated evidence to support those inputs.

If you're ready to begin confronting your business problem, then it's time to begin applying Six Sigma. The DMAIC (define-measure-analyze-improve-control) methodology is the heart of Six Sigma. These are the Six Sigma steps for your improvement project. The starting point is obvious—Define. You will notice that this phase integrates everything we've talked about up to this point, because in the Define phase you'll confirm the preliminary decisions you made about the reasons for tackling the problem you identified and go into more detail about the purpose, objectives, and scope of your project. You'll also collect data on the process and your customers and identify the project results you want. In other words, by the end of this phase, you will have effectively defined your project. By now, you should have chosen your first project and you should be ready to begin moving into DMAIC.

When to Do the Training

As discussed in Chapter 4, there are a lot of options for the training that people in your company will receive. The timing is also flexible. You may choose to have a Black Belt or a Green Belt trained and then launch a project. You may choose to require that candidates lead a project as part of their training. You may choose to complete the scoping of the project before beginning the formal education of the Belts in the project. The only wrong option would be to do the project first *and then* train your people! Otherwise, do what makes sense for your situation.

Overview of the Define Phase

Let's approach Define systematically. The following outline delineates the steps in the Define process. This outline is not written in stone; you can modify and adapt it to your requirements. However, it is important that you don't *eliminate* any steps.

1. Identify the problems in your process.

2. Identify the process owner/sponsor.

3. Begin the project charter.

4. Assemble the project team.

5. Build a RACI chart.

6. Collect customer data.

7. Translate VOC into CTQs.

8. Develop problem statements.

9. Establish project metrics.

10. Focus on the vital few factors.

11. Identify necessary resources.

12. Create a project plan.

13. Conduct a Phase-Gate Review.

It is almost a given, however, that you'll have to translate the description of actors and roles in this improvement drama to fit your situation. In the traditional Six Sigma deployment model, there are very specific responsibilities for very specific roles:

- The corporate **Champion** helps to choose the projects and oversees *all* projects.

- The manager most closely affected by the project acts as **Sponsor**, the person who monitors and reviews the team results, runs interference when needed to remove roadblocks, and makes sure the team has what it needs to succeed.

- The **team leader** would be a full-time **Black Belt**, who is getting training and coaching from a **Master Black Belt**.

- The remaining **team members** would be people from the affected work area, Green Belts or Yellow Belts if they have received some introductory training, but that's not always the case.

For a small business, these roles will likely shift. The Champion, who may be you or another executive, may also have to function as the Sponsor. You may have a Black Belt or someone training to be a Black Belt to act as the team leader or you may fill that role with a Green Belt or someone training to be a Green Belt who gets a lot of coaching from an outside expert, either a Black Belt or a Master Black Belt.

For the purposes of this chapter and the rest of the DMAIC chapters, I'll use the general terms *project sponsor* and *team leader*. But remember that the assumption is that a number of these people will be getting training in Six Sigma or have already completed training.

Step 1: Identify the Problems in Your Process

This step continues the thinking that went into selecting the project, as explained in Chapter 5. This is a preliminary process, to provide some initial focus. A little later in the Define phase the team will gather data that will allow it to sharpen its focus and develop the problem statement.

Step 2: Identify the Process Owner/Sponsor

The project Sponsor is often played by the *process owner*—the manager or supervisor who is closest to the process you are improving. It is important that the process owner either act as the Sponsor or be directly involved as the

> **Process owner** The person who has authority over how a process operates and ultimate responsibility for the results.

team leader or a team member, because his or her approval will be needed before any changes are made. The horror stories of teams whose recommendations were never implemented because the sponsor didn't approve are too many to recount here! (If the process owner is directly involved in the project, as the Black Belt leading the team, for example, then the process owner's boss should act as Sponsor.)

Let's assume that the process owner will function as a project Sponsor, which means that he or she is responsible for the following:

- Beginning and supporting the project
- Ensuring that all team members fully understand the project and are firmly committed to achieving the results
- Owning and ensuring implementation of the solution
- Removing all barriers to the project
- Being accountable for the performance and outcome of the project

Step 3: Begin the Project Charter

The project charter is a document that evolves over the course of a Six Sigma project. It names the project, lists the people involved and delineates the responsibilities of each, identifies the project objectives, links them to the organization's strategic goals, and establishes the reasons for the project.

The charter has its roots in your project-selection efforts. The project and objective statements you created in Chapter 5 represent the early stages of your project charter. Essentially, the charter documents a Six Sigma project and provides all relevant information about it. Anyone who reads this document should be able to understand all of the elements of a project. Choose a descriptive title: it should make the subject and purpose of your project immediately recognizable. We'll go into more detail about the charter later in this chapter.

Figure 6-1 shows an example of the project charter. At this point, the charter won't contain much information; team members will add to it and modify it as the project progresses.

Step 4: Assemble the Project Team

You've already identified the Champion, who will function as your *strategic* leader, and project Sponsor (most likely the process owner or the process owner's boss). The next step is to choose the team leader (prefer-

Project Team Charter	
Black Belt Name:	Champion Name:
Project Start Date:	Project Location:
Projected Complete Date:	

Business Case:

Problem Statement:

Project Objective:

Team Members:

Stakeholders:

Subject Matter Experts:

Constraints/Assumptions:

Scope Start Point:

Scope Ending Point:

Preliminary Plan: (attach to this form)

Black Belt Signoff:

Champion Signoff:

Figure 6-1. Project team charter

ably a Black Belt, a Green Belt, or an employee who is getting the required training to become a Black Belt or a Green Belt).

Once you have chosen the team leader, he or she and the Sponsor and the Champion should work together to assemble the rest of the Six Sigma team. Typically, an ideal team size is five to seven people, though a smaller team (three or four people) works if the project focus is very narrow. Empirically, five to seven has worked well because it's enough people to represent diverse viewpoints and opinions, but not so big that the team bogs down in its own complexity!

Whom should you choose as team members?

- You'll want at least a few people who have some knowledge of the process being studied. (If these people are Green or Yellow Belts, so much the better; the exposure to Six Sigma methods is often helpful in their development.)

- If you know that a particular area of expertise will be needed in the project (such as financial, marketing, or technical knowledge), assign someone with the appropriate background to the team.

- As noted in Chapter 4, I strongly recommend including a customer and/or a supplier on the team, especially if the problem relates to a specific customer or supplier. Asking these people to participate on the team speaks volumes about your company's commitment to serve the customer better or to support a long-term relationship with the supplier.

Ideally, you should select people who will work well together, keeping in mind the personalities of the individuals involved. If your organization is small, however, your choices will be limited. If there are personality conflicts, it is the Champion's job to resolve them.

Experts Can Also "Consult" the Team

Not everyone who has something to contribute to a team need be a full-fledged team member. Often it's just as effective (and a lot more efficient) to have people with a particular expertise or viewpoint attend just a few team meetings where their knowledge is needed. That way they are there when it most helps the team, but they don't have to attend all the team meetings or participate in other team activities (like data collection). For example, someone from finance must be involved in validating both the opportunity (when the project starts) and the results (when the project ends), but that doesn't mean that a financial expert should be assigned to the team.

> **Don't Just Take Whoever Is Available!**
> The absolute worst criterion for choosing a team member is the person happens to have the time. Better to have a smaller team or delay the project altogether if people with the right knowledge or background aren't available. Better yet, shift their responsibilities so they *are* available!

When putting your team together, think about what happens after the project is completed—implementation. Remember that *everyone* in the organization should be involved in the implementation. Everyone should know what's going on, the goals for the project, and the other essentials.

Step 5: Build a RACI Chart

Once you have assembled your team, the next step is to determine how involved each member will be in the decision-making process. The best way to do that is to create a system chart according to the RACI (pronounced ray-see) model. RACI stands for:

- **Responsibility**—people who will actively participate and contribute as much as possible

- **Accountability**—the person who will ultimately be responsible for the project results

- **Consultation**—people who will be consulted, because they have either some expertise or some authority

- **Inform**—people who will be affected by any decisions made and will have to be informed

The RACI chart is a very effective tool. It documents involvement and responsibilities, establishes ownership, and unites the team. In essence, the chart functions as a contract. It helps avoid conflict and confusion by identifying the people who will be affected by the project and how best to work with them. Figure 6-2 shows what a RACI chart might look like for the company that almost failed because of its marketing problem.

Once you have created your RACI chart, the team leader should assemble the team for a kickoff meeting, the official start of the Six Sigma project.

	Activities							
Team Members	**Identify Needs for Outside Guru**	**Selecting Outside Expert**	**Selecting Growth Projects**	**Project Work**	**Team Support**	**Driving Growth Project**	**Install Solution**	**Sustain Gain**
Executive Team	R	R	R	I	I	I	I	I
Champion	R	I	I	R	R	R	R	R
Finance	I	C	I	I	I	I	I	A
Marketing	R	C	R	A	R	A	R	A
Black Belt	C	C	A	A	R	A	R	R
Team Members		C	C	C	C	C	C	C
Expert			R	R	A	R	A	A

Figure 6-2. Sample RACI chart

Step 6: Collect Customer Data

The first thing the team members should do after the kickoff is to identify all of the customers who will be affected by your project. Once they have done that, they will then determine those customers' needs and expectations (*critical requirements*).

Critical requirements (aka critical-to-quality requirements, CTQs) The features or performance characteristics that are most important to customers.

It's crucial to do this right: it's the basis for the whole project. Do the CTQs wrong and it doesn't matter how well you do everything else.

There was a famous problem solver named Dorian Shainin who would say, "You need to talk to the part to get the information you need." What he meant was that you need to talk to the process or really observe the defects. In the Six Sigma world, this method is known as "Be the Customer": you step into the shoes of the process, part, or transaction to understand and observe what really goes on from that point of view. It's the old *Caddyshack* line about golfing: "Just be the ball, be the ball, be the ball."

Capturing and translating the customer's needs is critical to ensuring the Define phase focus for each development project. This includes deciding how to identify end customers and which customers to contact in order to capture their requirements. As customers are identified, suitable techniques are used to assemble the Voice of the Customer (VOC), telling us what customers value.

VOC means listening to what your customers are telling you they care about. It is customer requirements as defined by the customer, not by marketing or sales or manufacturing or a manager.

For example, I was taking my family on a drive to drop my son off at a YMCA mountain camp and my mother said, "I wish they would let me design the air conditioner for cars because those men designers have never taken the loudness into consideration!" The voice of that customer was that air conditioner volume was an important characteristic!

There is no monolithic voice of the customer. Customer voices are diverse. In consumer markets, there are a variety of needs. Even within one buying unit, there are multiple customer voices (e.g., children and parents). This also applies to industrial and government markets. There are even multiple customer voices within a single organization.

How do you collect this valuable VOC data? There are many ways. Here are two common approaches:

1. Use existing data, such as customer complaints

2. Gather new data

In general, existing data is OK to use as a baseline or to get a general sense of the context of the problem. But you should never base decisions solely on old data. You have to gather new VOC data directly related to the problem or issue you're studying.

So, how do you gather data about your customers? Here are some options:

- Telephone survey
- Mail survey
- Focus group, either online or in person
- One-on-one interviews
- Intercept interviews (on the street, for example)
- Observation of the customer using the product or service

The first options on this list—telephone and mail surveys—are best used to gather a lot of quantitative information quickly, such as when you want to verify the demand for a particular service or feature. They work well when you use *close-ended questions,* those with just a few options from which respondents choose.

> **Close-ended question**
> Question for which the answers are limited to selecting from a list (options A to E, "don't care" to "care a lot," etc.). Survey questions are typically close-ended.
>
> **Open-ended question**
> Question for which there is no predefined set of answers. Customers are free to answer any way they choose, using any words they choose.

Focus groups and interviews are better used for qualitative data, when you ask *open-ended questions* and customers can respond any way they want. Observation is the preferred method if you're involved in designing or redesigning a product or service, because often customers can't put their needs or frustrations into words, so surveys or interviews won't get you the kind of information you need.

Here are some questions you need to answer no matter what type of data you're going to collect:

1. How will we collect the information?
2. What data do we need?
3. Where is the end customer going to use the product or service?
4. When is the end customer going to use the product or service?
5. How will we use the information?
6. What customer problem are we trying to solve?

   Whatever method(s) you choose, be sure to follow these guidelines:

   • If you can't contact all the customers affected by the project, make sure the sample you choose is representative of the entire customer segment or population.

   • Select participants at random.

   • Close-ended survey questions should be objective and easily converted into quantitative data.

   • In focus groups and interviews, you will likely use mostly open-ended questions, but you may want to include a few close-ended survey-type questions so you'll have some quantitative results as well.

Think from the Customers' Perspective

Surveys should be written from a customers' point of view, not yours. Include customers in designing the questions. You don't learn much from simple yes or no questions, so try to use questions where the optional answers lie along a scale. Scaling helps define the focus. A useful scale to use is a Likert scale (invented by Rensis Likert in 1932), which is a 1-to-5 rating scale. The lowest rating—1—is unacceptable and the highest rating—5—is excellent. The sample size to determine the number of surveys needed is an extremely important factor. A rule of thumb for sample size is $n \times p \geq 5$ percent, where n is the sample size and p is the percentage of probability of a defect or problem occurring.

Suppose, for example that five out of every 100 hotel guests get a room with a dirty bathtub. You divide the number of possible dirty bathtubs (100) by the number of actual dirty bathtubs (four) to get a probability of 25 percent. The proper sample size (n) for this problem, using the formula $n \geq 5 \times 25$ ($100 \div 4$), would be 125. There is no value to the survey if the sample size is not calculated.

Step 7: Translate VOC into CTQs

Once you have collected the Voice of the Customer, you need to translate what you've learned into how it relates to the product or service that's the subject of the project. What you want to know is what's most important to the customer, what's critical to quality.

The level of sophistication needed to reach CTQ definitions that are useful to the project will vary by situation. Here are three optional paths, in order from simplest to most complex.

CTQ Path 1: Customer Prioritization

The simplest path to finding what's important to customers is to ask them to rank or rate features or aspects of your product or service. The ranking (first, second, third, and so forth) or rating (5 = very important, 1 = not important at all) is critical, because you want to be able to judge the *relative* importance of the features or aspects. That's the only way you'll be able to make the trade-off decisions you'll inevitably face later in the project.

CTQ Path 2: The YX Matrix

You can be much more specific and quantitative about defining CTQs by creating a YX matrix, like the example in Figure 6-3 (next page), which shows how factors related to coffee making relate to desired outcomes.

The terminology comes from the transfer function introduced earlier in this book, that $Y = f(X)$, "Y is a function of X." In the matrix you list the important outputs (Y's) across the top and potential drivers or X's down the side and evaluate how much each X factor affects the output (that's the "Association" area in the figure).

The final rankings are calculated by multiplying the individual "association" ratings by the customer priority ranks, then summing to get a total for each factor. In this example, Coffee Type ranks first, with a score of 320, which results from the following math: $(10 \times 10) + (10 \times 10) + (10 \times 10) + (2 \times 10) = 320$.

CTQ Path 3: Quality Function Deployment and the House of Quality

The YX matrix belongs to a larger set of tools collectively known as *Quality Function Deployment* (QFD). Also known as the *House of Quality*, QFD focuses on achieving customer satisfaction using measures such as customer retention. QFD focuses on delivering value by looking for the Voice of the Customer (both expressed and unexpressed), converting the VOC into tasks, features, designs, and communicating these throughout the company to start the satisfaction process. In addition, QFD has an output to prioritize requirements, benchmark those requirements against competitors, and then finally point the company to optimize those items of the process, product, or service that will result in the greatest competitive edge.

The structure of the full House of Quality is shown in Figure 6-4 (page 98).

These are the elements of the House:

- **Customer requirements** (hows)—a structured list of requirements derived from customer statements.

- **Technical requirements** (whats)—a structured set of relevant and measurable product characteristics.

	1	2	3	4	5	6	7
(Y) Variable Customer Output	Taste	Aroma	Price	Acidity			
Priority Customer Rank	10	10	10	2			
Key Process Input X-Variable			**Association Table**				
Coffee Type	10	10	10	10			
Amt. of Coffee	9	7	1	1			
Grind Time	9	6	20	80			
Water Temp.	9	3	2	2			
Cup Type	2	4	4	2			
Cup Size	2	4	5	1			
Brew Time	9	6	2	2			

Customer Key Process Input Variable	Rank	%	Customer Key Process Ouput Variable	Customer Priority Rank #
Coffee Type	320	24.43%	Taste	10
Amt. of Coffee	280	21.37%	Aroma	10
Grind Time	176	13.44%	Price	10
Water Temp.	144	10.99%	Acidity	2
Cup Type	104	7.94%		
Cup Size	112	8.55%		
Brew Time	174	13.28%		

Figure 6-3. Sample YX matrix for making coffee

- **Planning matrix**—an illustration of customer perceptions observed in market surveys, including the relative importance of customer requirements and of the performance of the company and competitors toward meeting these requirements.

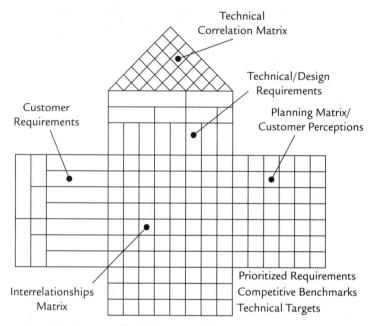

Figure 6-4. The house of quality
Source: developed by Dr. Antony Lowe in collaboration with Professor Keith Ridgway, University of Sheffield, England.

- **Interrelationship matrix**—an illustration of the QFD team's perceptions of interrelationships between technical and customer requirements.

- **Technical correlation matrix**—a grid where the team identifies how technical requirements support or impede each other in the product design and highlights innovation opportunities.

- **Technical priorities, benchmarks, and targets**—an area where the team records the priorities assigned to technical requirements by the matrix, measures of technical performance achieved by competitive products and the degree of difficulty involved in developing each requirement.

For the interrelationship matrix at the heart of the House, the team applies an appropriate scale, illustrated with symbols or figures. The team discusses the factors and decides on the value of each interrelationship by consensus; this process can be time-consuming. To reduce the demands on resources, the team can concentrate on key relationships and minimize the number of requirements.

The final output of the matrix is a set of target values for each technical requirement to be met by the new design, values linked to the demands of the customer.

An example of a simplified completed House of Quality is shown in Figure 6-5.

The QFD or House of Quality has become a critical tool for Design

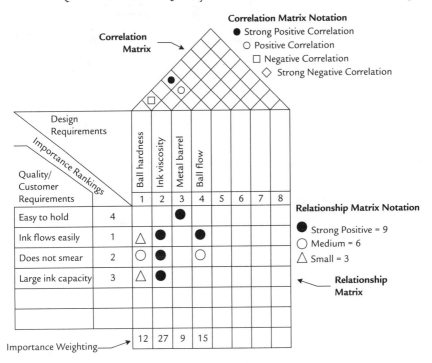

Figure 6-5. Simplified House of Quality, for a pen manufacturer

for Six Sigma as well. It serves the purpose of displaying complex Y = f (X) transfer functions, where Y is the critical-to-customer-satisfaction factors and X is the critical-to-quality factors. There can be multiple layers, starting with a product or service and going

Design for Six Sigma A methodology used to prevent problems in a process. It uses many of the same tools and techniques as Six Sigma, such as QFD and the House of Quality.

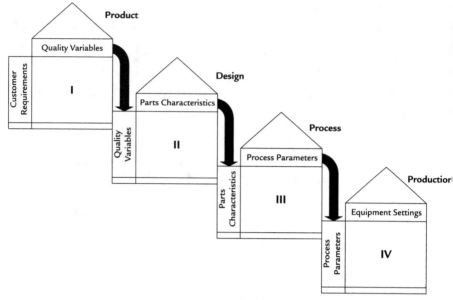

Figure 6-6. Layered House of Quality used in QFD

through design and process to production or internal operational requirements. This layering is used to link the customer requirements to the factors inside the company to ensure satisfaction, as depicted in Figure 6-6.

In the Define phase, the purpose of using the VOC is to ensure that the customer requirements are linked to the inputs that drive the desired result.

Step 8: Develop Problem Statements

At the start of the Define phase the team identified the problems with the process. Then, it gathered the VOC and determined the customer CTQs. At this point it should define, as specifically as it can, where and when and in what ways the product or service fails to meet those CTQs. These are opportunities for improvement! It should use any quantitative data it has on hand. Such data is often suspect because the team hasn't yet studied procedures for measuring the process, but it can provide a general idea of the variation and scope of the problems. The team will be collecting new data in the Measure phase to verify its conjectures. For each problem, the team members develop a statement. It is extremely important to define each problem specifically and in quantitative terms.

> In 80 percent of projects that fail, the reason is that they are not defined properly.

Your problem statement should answer the following questions:

- What is the problem?
- What is the current status of the process?
- What do you think needs to be done to change the process? (You won't know for sure until after you get through the Analyze phase of DMAIC.)
- How long will it take to make the necessary changes?
- How much money will it save?

Step 9: Establish Project Metrics

After determining your customer CTQs, the next step is to establish the metrics to be used to monitor and evaluate progress in this project. These metrics should reflect both the VOC and the business goals and objectives. Remember that you must always link the metrics to the company's strategic goals! Also, it is OK to challenge the strategic goals.

Be sure that the metrics are relevant to the problems identified, meaningful, within the scope of the project, and simple and straightforward enough that all team members understand them easily and in the same way.

Step 10: Focus on the Vital Few Factors

Now it is time for the team to determine the vital few components of the problem. Keep in mind that Six Sigma is surgical. You can't address *all* aspects of the problem in one project! Using a Pareto analysis, you will focus on the most important components—those that cause the biggest share of the observed problems.

Do you remember the discussion of the Pareto Principle in Chapter 5? Here's the time to apply the three tiers of Pareto analysis if you haven't done so already.

Begin with your definition of the problem and then list the potential components of a specific effect. List no more than eight to ten. Collect data to create a Pareto chart and focus on the vital few factors that are the biggest troublemakers.

Figure 6-7 shows the results for the coffee example from the YX matrix discussion. There are many ways to show the data in both tabular and graphic formats. The key is to use the simplest visual to convey the message to the audience. People learn in various ways, so presenting the concept in different ways helps them learn.

Customer Key Process Input Variable	Rank	%
Coffee Type	320	24.43%
Amt. of Coffee	280	21.37%
Grind Time	176	13.44%
Brew Time	144	10.99%
Water Temp.	104	7.94%
Cup Type	112	8.55%
Cup Size	174	13.28%

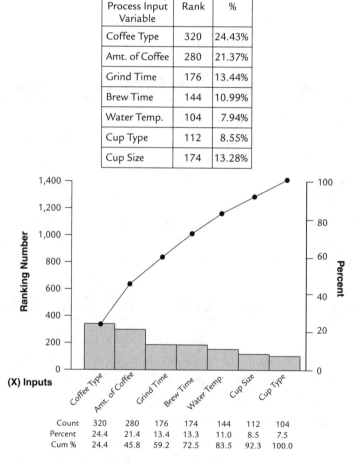

	Count	Percent	Cum %
Coffee Type	320	24.4	24.4
Amt. of Coffee	280	21.4	45.8
Grind Time	176	13.4	59.2
Brew Time	174	13.3	72.5
Water Temp.	144	11.0	83.5
Cup Size	112	8.5	92.3
Cup Type	104	7.5	100.0

Figure 6-7. Pareto chart depicting input variables

Step 11: Identify Necessary Resources

At this stage, it is necessary to determine what resources will be needed to carry out the project. You, the Executive Leader, your Champion, the Sponsor, and the team leader (Black Belt or substitute!) should consult with a member of your financial department to identify these resources. These would include money, administrative support, and training.

Step 12: Create a Project Plan

It is important to create a detailed plan for your project. The plan should consist of steps, scheduled milestones, deliverables, and goals for each of the five DMAIC phases of the project. Working together, your Champion and Black Belt (and you, if you choose), should create this plan. The project plan should ensure that your project stays focused and on track. Your plan should include the following components:

- **Milestones.** These are checkpoints that indicate when and where the team should be in the project. At each milestone the Black Belt will report to the Champion on the team's progress and any problems it has encountered.

- **Tasks.** The plan should specify the person who has primary responsibility for each task.

- **Checklist of tools.** For each task there should be a list of assigned tools.

- **Communications plan.** This should specify items to be communicated (such as project status reports, minutes of team meetings, etc.), who will be communicating each item (Champion, Black Belt, Green Belt, etc.), and to whom each item will be communicated (team members, executive leaders, etc.). It should also indicate when the information will be communicated (specific dates or frequency), how the information will be transmitted (memo, e-mail, telephone call, presentation, etc.), and where the information will be stored for future reference.

Step 13: Conduct a Phase-Gate Review

At the end of each phase of the DMAIC process, the Black Belt should report to the executive leaders on the status of the project. This *phase-gate review* (also known as a *Six Sigma review*) will give you, the Executive Leader, the chance to ask questions, make suggestions, address any problems, allocate additional resources, etc. It is also an opportunity for you to provide support and emphasize your commitment to the project. This review will ensure that the team stays focused and the project stays on track.

Keep Presentations Short

A good method for conducting these reviews is to restrict the presentation to 15 minutes: ten minutes to report on the project and five minutes to answer questions. Usually, information provided in the report answers most questions, so five minutes should be sufficient. If the Black Belt's presentation is mainly a story line with few graphs and charts, this is an indication that he or she wasted time and did not put effort into the project.

Conclusion

At the end of the Define phase, you should have the following:

1. A documented project defined with a clear goal and objective
2. Resources identified (the team)
3. A sense of direction to focus the project team
4. A basic plan
5. CTQs
6. A problem statement for each problem
7. A clear understanding of the adverse effect of the defect to the customer

Summary of the Major Steps in the Define Phase

1. Identify the problems in the process.
2. Identify the process owner/sponsor.

3. Begin the project charter.

4. Assemble the project team.

5. Build a RACI chart.

6. Collect customer data and identify the customers who will be affected by the project.

7. Translate VOC into CTQs.

8. Develop problem statement(s). Problem statements should answer the following questions:

   • What is the problem?

   • What is the current status of the process?

   • What needs to be done to change the process?

   • How long will it take to make the necessary changes?

   • How much money will it save?

9. Establish the project metrics.

10. Focus on the vital few factors.

11. Identify necessary resources.

12. Create a project plan.

13. Conduct a phase-gate review (Six Sigma review).

6σ
SB

Chapter 7

Your Six Sigma Project: The Measure Phase

Remember, a real decision is measured by the fact that you've
taken new action. If there's no action, you haven't truly decided.
—Anthony Robbins

I do take action, but the measurements I use are full of errors! My name
is Richard Wise, and I am the president of a medium-size heating,
ventilation, and air conditioning business in the Northwest United
States. We took many new actions on data that was not valid. I was reading about Six Sigma and decided to consult with an expert to assess our
situation.

After the assessment, I was shocked to find our operations were full
of unrecognized defects, resulting in too many wasted dollars. Our expert
called it the "hidden factory" or the inherent waste that we basically considered just part of the way our processes work. I knew at that moment
we had to make changes. The Measure phase was very enlightening for
me. It's hard to share the dirty laundry we uncovered. It is this phase that
changed my attitude about the necessity of making decisions with valid
data before taking any new actions.

To make the point, here is an example of some real dirty laundry. We scheduled our production based on orders from the field and worked overtime to ensure that our installation met the contractors' move-in dates. Our measure of success was on-time delivery to the field-requested order. We were 93 percent successful as measured by the field, but only 73 percent on time according to our contractors. *Why?* We did not measure returns from the field due to damaged parts, wrong parts, missing parts, special kits missing, or wrong parts built. There was 15 to 23 days of inventory in our outside scrap area, which did not include on-site storage scrap areas. The field-request data was not valid from the contractors' point of view, and they were requesting rework of parts that had already been manufactured and delivered because we did not measure our *returns*!

To make a point to our company, I stated that we were basically manufacturing three weeks straight for the waste disposal facility. Our measurement of on-time delivery needed to include scrap and rework for the field request. The cost of three weeks of production and materials was well over $1.5 million in pure profit. This cost of the waste was 18 percent of our total profit. What Six Sigma taught me was that all measurements *must* first be valid prior to using the data for any decisions and to set a baseline for the problem.

This is a typical story and the problem is common in businesses of all sizes and in all types of industries. Companies need to validate measurements for data to be used in making decisions. The Measure phase ensures you have a good working measurement system, so you can trust the data that you are going to analyze. What Richard was measuring as a key business metric was fine, but the basis of the measurement and the error or variation in the measurement from the two perspectives were wrong!

The Measure phase of Six Sigma has two components:

1. Validate the measurement system (making sure you can trust the numbers).
2. Collect new data.

I'll outline a specific series of steps for Measure later in this chapter, but first I want to talk about what it means to validate a measurement system and why it's so important.

Can You Trust Your Data?

The goal of this first part of the Measure phase is to make sure you have valid data. What does it mean to be *valid*?

Suppose you were to measure your height at home and then again at the doctor's office. You get different results. Which measurement would you trust? Why? When you check out at the grocery store, do you trust the cash register to give you an accurate total? The receipt you get is a measurement, but is it valid? These are simple things that we assume are correct.

However, you are about to be sensitized to a new reality that will shock you—*many measurement systems don't produce good data.*

Case 1: Grocery Store Receipts

Let's get specific with the grocery receipt example. The receipt is a measurement of the grocery store's sales process. The receipt must be *accurate*, which means that it correctly represents the sales of the items purchased every time. The receipt must also be *precise*, which means that the figures must be specific enough: if the cash registers calculate dollars but not cents, there's a problem. You can have a precise receipt that is inaccurate or wrong; in other words it is consistently wrong.

> **Accurate** Term describing results that are true or correct.
>
> **Precise** Term describing results that are sufficiently specific.
>
> **Repeatable** Term describing results that are the same when the same person uses the measurement system two or more times on a given item.
>
> **Reproducible** Term describing results that are the same when two or more people use the measurement system on a given item.

If we really want to know if the receipt measurement is valid, we must be able to repeat it over and over and over and get the same result each time (that is, the measurement is *accurate* and *repeatable*).

Here's an example. You go TO the grocery store and buy items that add up to $98.54, a figure that you determine is accurate. You then take the same items to two more cashiers and have them run those items through their scanners. To get a simple measure of repeatability, you ask each of the three cashiers to do the same thing all over again, so you have six measurements (three cashiers, two measurements each). If the scanners and cashiers were operating with the same methods, you would expect that you'd get a total of $98.54 six times.

If you have never tried this, you will be surprised to find that seven percent of the time there will be a difference. Why? Because the measurement system has errors! This example, using different shoppers with the same list of items purchased and repurchased at different times (with the permission of the store management), resulted in the data shown in Figure 7-1.

Cashier	Total Price
1	$98.54
1	$92.21
2	$98.54
2	$91.59
3	$97.74
3	$97.74

Figure 7-1. Testing the validity of measurements: grocery prices

As you can see in Figure 7-1, only cashier number three was able to get a repeatable total price—but that price was not accurate! The other two cashiers were not able to get a repeatable price, but each of them was accurate once.

So the first problem is that this system of measurement has repeatability problems. The second problem is *reproducibility*—the measurement system's ability to reproduce the measurement among two or more operators or, in this example, cashiers. Except for the two accurate measurements, no readings from the three cashiers are the same.

Using Gage R&R to Create a Valid Measurement System

This simple example illustrates the basics of a set of techniques known as *measurement system analysis* (MSA). This particular method is called *gage R&R*.

Gage R&R A technique for determining the validity of a measurement system according to four essential criteria: accuracy, repeatability, reproducibility, and stability (accuracy, repeatability, and reproducibility over time).

By convention, a full gage R&R usually requires at least 60 measurement points, which in this case would require three cashiers getting two measurements each of ten grocery carts that represent the normal buying scenario.

Do repeatability and reproducibility really matter? How would this adversely affect your customers and the grocery store?

- You are unknowingly overpricing or underpricing the customer.
- You are unknowingly producing accounting errors resulting in a variance to actual sales.

Unless you've studied your measurement system, you don't know the magnitude of the error. This example was only six transactions; it could be representative of possibly hundreds of transactions every day, which can lead to a major problem across your chain of stores. Not knowing is the real problem—and taking it for granted that your measurements are valid is absolutely wrong. The Measure phase is where we begin to know what we don't know.

Know How Your System Works

Do not forget that Six Sigma is about solving problems in your business process. What will set you apart in business is knowing how your system works and how the processes in your system work together to deliver value to your customer.

I was consulting for a rubber glove manufacturing business that required that the industrial gloves it was shipping had no defects. In the final inspection process, about 27 percent of the gloves were rejected because defects were found. Those defects were costing approximately $20,000 per week. My standard joke with my clients about inspection is that they should inspect only the good ones! Of course, if we knew which were the good ones, we would not have to test or inspect.

The point is not to inspect, but expect! I wanted to perform a simple validation of the inspection process, so I grabbed 200 pairs of gloves that were rejected and secretly put them through the system with a small, unnoticeable identifying mark for tracking. Out of the 200 gloves, 78 were now deemed good and were shipped to the customer. What my test showed was the inspectors didn't know what a defect was or was not. I ran this test three more times and tracked the inspectors to see who was judging good and bad gloves. Three out of the ten inspectors were finding three times more defects than the other inspectors. After a basic investigation, the key distinguishing factor for these three inspectors was that they wore no eyeglasses. A simple eye exam determined that they needed glasses. The defect rate went down by 30 percent and resulted in savings of $8,000 per week and less paid overtime for production, saving the company over $375,000.

The glove example clearly demonstrates the difference between a valid measurement and an invalid measurement. The inspection process was not working; it was defective. This inspection was not a true indicator of the process that made the gloves and therefore could cause wrong decisions to be made on a process. You are making judgments based on defects, so you need to ensure a valid measurement system. *Do not assume you know how to measure!*

Case 2: Loan Application Evaluation

Let's use a bank example to show that measurements for transactional processes must be valid as well. The bank was processing simple loan applications daily. The measurement was making "accept or reject" judgments on loan applications. We performed a simple study called an *attribute study*. (An attribute is a characteristic that cannot be put on a linear scale: it's yes or no, right or wrong, with no degrees of difference.) Here's how the study worked.

Step 1. We pulled 30 applications that were categorized into two groups: rejected and accepted. We used three of the top loan officers (the gurus of the loan application world) to determine these two groups.

Step 2. We took these 30 applications to 12 loan processors and had them determine which should be accepted and which should be rejected.

Step 3. We then analyzed the results. We found that seven processors out of 12 were judging the applications the same as the gurus. This meant that more than 40 percent of the measurement system was judging the applications incorrectly.

Valid applications were being rejected and invalid applications were being accepted. Almost half the people in the loan department were causing rework because they did not have a common and accurate measure of the distinction between unacceptable and acceptable.

It was costing the bank both by wasting the time of its resources and by upsetting applicants—potential customers. An applicant that you have wrongly rejected will simply go to another bank. The price your bank pays for this mistake is both lost business and a tarnished reputation.

Validate Your Measurements

The two cases above show how you can improve the quality of your measurement system no matter whether you're dealing with numeric data (like the grocery store receipts) or judgment data (like accepting or rejecting loan applications).

Overview of the Measure Phase

Now that you understand the basics of validation, we can outline the steps required in the Measure phase:

1. Select product or process CTQ characteristics; e.g., CTQ Y's.
2. Define performance standards for Y's.
3. Identify X's.
4. Validate the measurement system for Y's and X's.
5. Collect new data.
6. Establish process capability (sigma level) for creating Y.
7. Conduct a phase-gate review.

You began step 1 when you worked on defining the project. Now you want to select the Y's—the results you want. You can't move on to step 4 without a clear, rationally defined performance standard for the Y's. That's your objective, how you will be measuring success.

Steps 1 and 3: Select Y's and Identify X's

We will start by discussing Steps 1 and 3 at once. Why? Because the Y's depend on the X's. So it makes sense to talk about identifying the focus Y's and identifying the X's that drive them. Then we'll discuss defining performance standards for those Y's.

You might recall from Chapter 2 the concept of the Y's and X's in the Six Sigma representation of the problem. These Y's are the key characteristics of the process you're trying to understand and improve or the problem you are trying to solve. The Y's are *dependent* variables because they depend on X's, which are *independent* variables.

Remember the transfer function: $Y = f(X)$. If we change that X, we can change that Y. The end goal for the Measure phase is to start understanding all of the potential X's that are affecting your processes and how well they perform—the Y's that result.

Profit for your business is a Y, a variable that is totally dependent on many X's, such as advertising, product quality and availability, service, cost controls, resource utilization, and so on. To change your Y, we need to change one or more of those X's.

The Y's that the grocery store was targeting for a Six Sigma improvement were total sales per hour (TS/hr), total items per hour (TI/hr), and correct total sales on every basket of items sold. The next step is to identify the X's on which those Y's depend. Don't assume that you know the X's!

I spoke with someone about the grocery store example and the Y of TS/hr and this person stated, "This is a silly measurement because everyone knows that this measurement only depends on the number of people coming into the store." *Wrong!* Yes, that's one of the X's, but the major X's that stood out were the number of cashiers available, the speed of the cashiers, the prices being correct, the availability of stockers, the status of equipment (working or broken), the availability of managers for approval, special promotions, and the stocking of items on the shelves. So, if you assume that total sales per hour depends only on the number of people who come into your store, you do not maximize your potential. The lesson: never assume knowledge!

Step 2: Define Performance Standards for Y's

As you look at your processes and identify the key outputs (Y's that should relate to the CTQs) and drivers or inputs (X's), you also need to think about what level of performance you want to achieve for both, but especially the Y's. For the grocery store, the goal might be to have no more than one inaccurate receipt for every 100 or every 1,000. The bank loan staff might want to set a goal of rejecting no loans that should be accepted.

Step 4: Validate the Measurement System for Y's and X's

This step should feel familiar to you; it's how we started this chapter. This is measurement system analysis. In simple terms, you do whatever it takes to make sure that your system of measurement produces data on your Y's and X's that is valid. The results must be:

- **Accurate**—true or correct
- **Precise**—sufficiently specific
- **Repeatable**—the same when the same person uses the measurement system two or more times on a given item
- **Reproducible**—the same when two or more people use the measurement system on a given item

How you validate the measurement system depends, of course, on the system and on the Y's and X's. The examples earlier in this chapter showed in simple terms how a grocery store and a bank worked to validate their measurement systems. The process isn't complicated, but it must be logical. Focus on these two questions:

- What things do you need to measure?
- How do you need to measure those things to get information that will allow you to evaluate your measurement system and ensure that it will produce results that you can use?

Step 5: Collect New Data

Have you ever done any painting in your house or taught a class? If so, you know that the prep work takes at least three or four times the effort of the actual execution. Data collection is often like that; but it's the planning and prep that ensure that the data you'll be collecting will be useful.

> **Make It Easy**
>
> When you are designing, creating, and installing new methods of data collection, it should *not* be viewed as a huge barrier within the company. It is OK to use a check sheet or a simple spreadsheet to get the needed data. It typically takes only a few seconds to collect data at the end of a process or transaction.

You've identified the Y's and X's for which you want to collect data and you've used the guidelines given at the start of this chapter to validate your measurement system. Now it's time to collect data.

You should approach data collection as logically as you've approached improvement.

- Define clearly what will be measured.
- Decide how much data you need. Typically, you want a minimum of 30 measurements; in some cases you may need a lot more. This is something your Black Belts will learn about in their training.
- Develop forms and procedures for collecting the data.
- Establish the sample size. Use the rule of thumb from Chapter 6. More data is better. A simple rule is more than 30. There are more complex and mathematical techniques, but this will serve as a guideline.
- Develop the sampling plan. It must ensure capturing most of the possible events that can occur over time. Production, sales, and other activities show variations throughout a day, a week, or a month.
- Train all data collectors in the procedures.
- Test out the procedures and make any refinements. Make sure you're getting measurements that are valid—accurate, precise, repeatable, and reproducible.
- Collect the data.

Step 6. Establish Process Capability for Creating Y

As discussed in Chapter 3, process capability is the ability of a stable process to achieve certain results. It's a statistical measure of inherent variation.

There are two methods for evaluating process capability:

- Calculate a sigma level based on yield.

- Do a capability analysis.

Calculating Sigma Levels

First, you need to calculate your capability in terms of sigma. The higher the sigma, the better your system is performing in terms of costs, profit, and defect rates. Figure 7-2 shows sigma levels in terms of defects per million opportunities (DPMO) and the cost of poor quality. (We'll explain the meaning of sigma a little later in this chapter.)

Sigma Level	Defects per Million Opportunities	Cost of Poor Quality (% of Sales)
6 Sigma	3.4	<10%
5 Sigma	233	10%–15%
4 Sigma	6,210	15%–20%
3 Sigma	66,807	20%–30%
2 Sigma	308,537	30%–40%
1 Sigma	690,000	–

Figure 7-2. Sigma levels in terms of defects and cost

Let's go back to the grocery store example to demonstrate this step. In that situation, we had to first fix the broken measurement system. We did this by fixing a common scanner adjustment that was wrong and by adding a software routine to calculate checksums. This routine verified the number of items and the price of those items, providing a way to test for total items that would indicate an error code to the cashier. The store could then collect new data that it knew was valid.

The important Y metrics for the grocery store were total sales per hour (TS/hr), total items per hour (TI/hr), and correct total sales on every basket of items sold. To establish a standard, they started by collecting data for TS/hr, TI/hr, and correct totals per basket sold from 15 stores. The summary graphs (Figures 7-3 and 7-4) show the data for the TS/hr and TI/hr metrics.

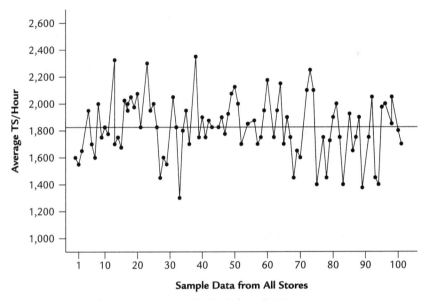

Figure 7-3. Total sales per hour (TS/hr) for all 15 stores

The third metric that the stores wanted to track was correct total for total number of baskets sold. This metric is a *discrete variable*, which means that a total is either correct or incorrect.

The discrete data can be considered a yield of successes in your process. Out of a sample of 1,000 baskets sold over a two-week period, we found 97 incorrect totals, which means an error rate of 9.7 percent (97 / 1,000). The yield is determined by subtracting the error rate from 100: 100 − 9.7 = 90.3 percent.

Now all we have to do is convert the yield of this process into sigma. At the end of this chapter is a sigma conversion table. Look up the yield in the first column and you'll find the corresponding sigma value in the second column.

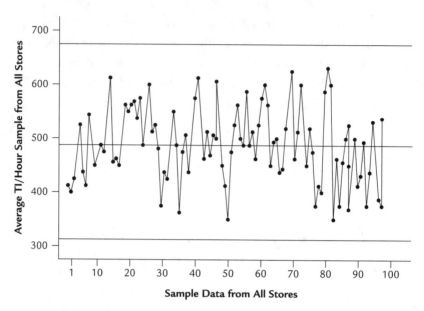

Figure 7-4. Total items per hour (TI/hr) for all 15 stores

<table>
<tr><td>

Continuous data Data readings that can theoretically fall anywhere along a continuum, which includes all physical and time measurements (weight, height, duration, density).

Discrete data Data readings for attributes (such as accept/reject, yes/no, right/wrong, acceptable/unacceptable).

</td></tr>
</table>

In this case the sigma level was 2.8σ (that's the Greek symbol for "sigma"), not very good. The store set the performance standard for this measure to achieve a 3.5σ (a yield of 97.7 percent) within three months. That improvement would mean saving an estimated $255,000 annually in rework expenses for accounting, inventory levels, customer service, and cashiers.

The table on the next page (Figure 7-5) compares sigma values in various industries. I would not recommend getting IRS advice by phone.

Process Capability Analysis

The other grocery store metrics—TS/hr and TI/hr—do not involve discrete variables. To determine the sigma value, we had to use a different method, *capability analysis*. This method compares actual performance of

Industies and Metrics	Defects per Million Opportunities	Sigma
IRS tax advice by phone	884,000	<.3
Wrong post-heart attack medications	420,500	1.7
Antibiotic overuse	135,000	2.7
Inpatient medical accuracy	66,000	3.0
Airline baggage handling	54,000	3.1
Preventable hospital deaths (total count ranges between 44,000 and 79,000)	4,661	4.1
Defective anesthesia during surgery	8.5	5.8
Domestic airline flight fatalities	1.3	6.2

Figure 7-5. Typical sigma levels in several industries
Source: GE Medical Systems, cited by Walter H. Ettinger, "Six Sigma: Adapting GE's Lessons to Health Care," *Trustee*, September 2001, p. 12

a process against performance standards, usually defined by *specification limits*, a term we used in Chapter 3.

Figure 3-2 showed a curve with two specification limits, the upper specification limit (USL) and the lower specification limit (LSL). Those boundaries distinguish between outputs that are OK and outputs that are not. For example, if an ideal delivery time is eight working hours, the customer may find anything between seven and nine acceptable: seven would be the LSL (nothing below that value is acceptable) and nine would be the USL (nothing above that value is acceptable).

> **Specification limits** Two values that represent the upper and lower boundaries of values that are acceptable to the customer.

Think of capability analysis in terms of a football player kicking the ball through the goal posts (which very physically define the specification limits). The grocery store needs to identify the goal posts or performance standards for the TS/hr and for the TI/hr. A typical guideline to use in setting a performance standard is to look for the best repetitive performance that you have demonstrated. Then put goal posts around that demonstrated capability.

The best internal performance that you have demonstrated over time is called your *level of entitlement*, because you've achieved it, therefore you are entitled to this level of performance. It's an achievable, realistic performance standard from which your business can begin the Six Sigma journey. For the TS/hr, the entitled goals were set at $2,100 as the LSL and $2,400 as the USL. This means that any sales/hour figure not between the goal posts of these standards is now considered a defect. Practically speaking, we know that above $2,400 is better, but let's make sure we are setting a stretch goal that is realistic. Of course, if we exceed the USL, that would be great.

> **Know What You Can Expect**
>
> Level of entitlement is a method to ensure that you set realistic goals. You take your critical business metrics over a cycle of time that shows most of the cycles of your process. You are looking for a pattern of excellence. A pattern is not a one-time event, but more than three times of occurrence. This pattern is your demonstrated internal level of entitlement, the performance that you can expect realistically.

Now that we have our standard, we can do the capability analysis. Let's first graph the data in a simple histogram (bar chart, Figure 7-6), which will help us examine the shape and spread of sample data for TS/hr. Histograms divide sample data points into many "buckets" called *intervals* or *bins*. The bars on the histogram represent the number of observations or count of occurrences of the data falling into each specified bin.

Here is where the capability analysis can determine the sigma value of this performance standard for the grocery store. The desired performance standard is $2,100-$2,400 in total sales per hour. The histogram shows that sales are generally between $1,100 and $2,500, significantly below the performance standard based on the level of entitlement.

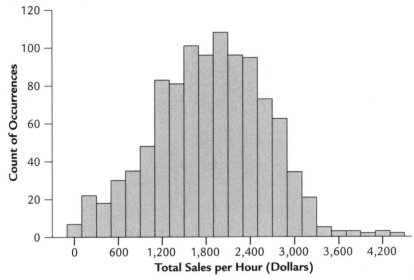

Figure 7-6. Histogram of total sales per hour

Capability Index

Process capability is commonly measured in terms of the capability index (Cp), which is a ratio without units. The purpose of this index is to assess whether a process, given its usual short-term variation, can meet established customer requirements or specifications. Cp is a ratio of the tolerance width (what is acceptable) to the short-term spread of the process (how much variation there is within a specific time period). You are basically dividing the performance standard (USL - LSL) by the process width.

$$Cp = \frac{\text{Performance Standard}}{\text{Performance Width}} \qquad Cp = \frac{USL - LSL}{6\sigma}$$

Process width is calculated as the spread of values within 6 sigma around the mean. Now we're getting into the basic meaning of *sigma: standard deviation.* Standard deviation is a measure of the variation of values from the mean (average): it's the average difference between any value in a set of values and the mean of all of the values in that set.

> **Standard deviation** A measure of the variation of values from the mean (average), the average difference between any value in a set of values and the mean of all of the values in that set.

How is standard deviation calculated? With software applications, fortunately, that use a formula that does the following for a process:

1. It finds the average of the values.

2. It subtracts the average from each of those values.

3. It squares the difference for each value (which makes any negative numbers positive).

4. It adds all of those squared deviation values.

5. It divides that sum of squared deviation values by the total number of values.

6. It takes the square root of the result of that division.

If the performance standard width is the same as the process width, this would result in an index of 1. A higher number is better. A lower number is a problem.

The Cp assumes that the mean is centered between the specification limits (normal curve), as shown in Figure 7-7.

The TS/hr histogram data (Figure 7-8) does *not* fit between the specification limits. It now is obvious that this performance is considered unacceptable. This is why we create performance standards.

The reason for calculating Cp with 6σ (standard deviations) is that if the values for a process are distributed equally on both sides of a given mean, the resulting curve is considered *normal* and 99.97 percent of the values are within 3 standard deviations (or $(3 - [-3]) = 6$) of the mean. So, if we can fit the process width between the specification limits, it means that 99.97 percent of the values are acceptable.

For the grocery stores, the standard deviation for total sales per hour is 641.5 for the values represented in the histogram (Figure 7-8). We multiply 641.5 (sigma) by 6 to get the process width: 3849. Then we plug that figure into the formula to calculate our capability index.

$$Cp = \frac{2,400 - 2,100}{3,849} = .07$$

What is left to do is to convert the Cp ratio for TS/hr of .07 into a sigma level. The sigma value (also referred to as Z) is simply ($3 \times$ Cp). This would make the sigma value for the TS/hr 0.21σ. If the goal is 6σ, the grocery store has a long way to go: $6 - 0.21 = 5.79$!

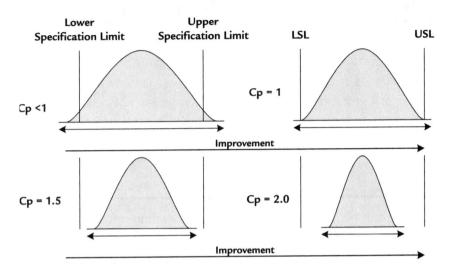

Figure 7-7. Normal curves and Cp ratios

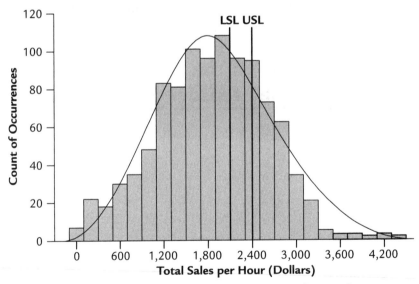

Figure 7-8. Histogram: process capabiility and specification limits

Now we are ready to move on to the Analyze phase, because we know all about our Y's and we have a list of potential X's. We now want to start understanding how those X's affect the problem we are trying to solve with the Y's.

Step 7: Conduct a Phase-Gate Review

At the end of the Measure phase, just as in the Define phase, the Black Belt should report to the executive leaders on the status of the project. This presentation is an opportunity for you to ask questions, make suggestions, address any problems, allocate additional resources, provide support, and show your commitment. The phase-gate review also ensures that the team stays focused and the project stays on track.

Conclusion

We have learned how not to assume that the measurement systems we use are valid until we test for repeatability and reproducibility. We need to ensure that we can reproduce the same measurement both between or among and within the measurement systems we are using. We have practiced how to convert data into sigma value for both discrete and variable data types. In some cases, if we fix the measurement system or install a data-collection system, the problem will be fixed.

Summary of the Major Steps in the Measure Phase

1. Select product or process CTQ characteristics.
2. Define performance standards for Y's.
3. Identify X's.
4. Validate the measurement system for Y's and X's.
5. Collect new data.
6. Establish process capability (sigma level) for creating Y's.
7. Conduct a phase-gate review.

Now we have arrived at the place where we know what we don't know and we feel humbled by our exposure. *Now we can start breaking down the problem with the Analyze phase!*

Sigma Abridged Conversion Table

Yield	Sigma Level	Defects per 1 Million	Defects per 100,000	Defects per 10,000	Defects per 1,000	Defects per 100
99.99966%	6.0	3.4	0.34	0.034	0.0034	0.00034
99.99946%	5.9	5.4	0.54	0.054	0.0054	0.00054
99.99915%	5.8	8.5	0.85	0.085	0.0085	0.00085
99.9987%	5.7	13	1.3	0.13	0.013	0.0013
99.9979%	5.6	21	2.1	0.21	0.021	0.0021
99.9968%	5.5	32	3.2	0.32	0.032	0.0032
99.9952%	5.4	48	4.8	0.48	0.048	0.0048
99.9928%	5.3	72	7.2	0.72	0.072	0.0072
99.989%	5.2	110	11	1.1	0.11	0.011
99.984%	5.1	160	16	1.6	0.16	0.016
99.977%	5.0	230	23	2.3	0.23	0.023
99.966%	4.9	340	34	3.4	0.34	0.034
99.952%	4.8	480	48	4.8	0.48	0.048
99.931%	4.7	690	69	6.9	0.69	0.069
99.903%	4.6	970	97	9.7	0.97	0.097
99.87%	4.5	1,300	130	13	1.3	0.13
99.81%	4.4	1,900	190	19	1.9	0.19
99.74%	4.3	2,600	260	26	2.6	0.26
99.65%	4.2	3,500	350	35	3.5	0.35
99.53%	4.1	4,700	470	47	4.7	0.47
99.38%	4.0	6,200	620	62	6.2	0.62
99.18%	3.9	8,200	820	82	8.2	0.82
98.9%	3.8	11,000	1,100	110	11	1.1
98.6%	3.7	14,000	1,400	140	14	1.4
98.2%	3.6	18,000	1,800	180	18	1.8
97.7%	3.5	23,000	2,300	230	23	2.3
97.1%	3.4	29,000	2,900	290	29	2.9
96.4%	3.3	36,000	3,600	360	36	3.6
95.5%	3.2	45,000	4,500	450	45	4.5
94.5%	3.1	55,000	5,500	550	55	5.5
93.3%	3.0	67,000	6,700	670	67	6.7
91.9%	2.9	81,000	8,100	810	81	8.1
90.3%	2.8	97,000	9,700	970	97	9.7
88%	2.7	120,000	12,000	1,200	120	12
86%	2.6	140,000	14,000	1,400	140	14
84%	2.5	160,000	16,000	1,600	160	16
82%	2.4	180,000	18,000	1,800	180	18
79%	2.3	210,000	21,000	2,100	210	21
76%	2.2	240,000	24,000	2,400	240	24
73%	2.1	270,000	27,000	2,700	270	27

Continued on the next page

Yield	Sigma Level	Defects per 1 Million	Defects per 100,000	Defects per 10,000	Defects per 1,000	Defects per 100
69%	2.0	310,000	31,000	3,100	310	31
66%	1.9	340,000	34,000	3,400	340	34
62%	1.8	380,000	38,000	3,800	380	38
58%	1.7	420,000	42,000	4,200	420	42
54%	1.6	460,000	46,000	4,600	460	46
50%	1.5	500,000	50,000	5,000	500	50
46%	1.4	540,000	54,000	5,400	540	54
42%	1.3	580,000	58,000	5,800	580	58
38%	1.2	620,000	62,000	6,200	620	62
34%	1.1	660,000	66,000	6,600	660	66
31%	2.0	690,000	69,000	6,900	690	69
27%	0.9	730,000	73,000	7,300	730	73
24%	0.8	760,000	76,000	7,600	760	76
21%	0.7	790,000	79,000	7,900	790	79
18%	0.6	820,000	82,000	8,200	820	82
16%	0.5	840,000	84,000	8,400	840	84
14%	0.4	860,000	86,000	8,600	860	86
12%	0.3	880,000	88,000	8,800	880	88
10%	0.2	900,000	90,000	9,000	900	90
8%	0.1	920,000	92,000	9,200	920	92
7%	0.0	930,000	93,000	9,300	930	93

Chapter 8

Your Six Sigma Project: The Analyze Phase

We can't solve problems by using the same kind of
thinking we used when we created them.
—Albert Einstein

D o you know the old tale of John Henry against the steam
engine, wondering which would win? Here's a real life example, a story of a little engine that did not make it.

The company was a small sand-casting company dating back to the
mid-1800s. It made wheels for the railroad industry for over a century
using tried-and-true methods. A decision was made to invest in a new
technology.

This decision is similar to decisions made by so many small businesses that are now investing in IT solutions. We make a decision to invest
and change our process in hopes of increasing our profit. How do we
know if this decision is right?

This is where the Analyze phase of the DMAIC begins! I was present
at the time of this technology shift and recognized the mistake that was
happening. Half the investment had already been made in the new technology. The sales pitch for the new technology was that it would reduce
labor, rework, and finishing quality *by more than half*. But the contract had

no performance standards, so the promised benefits of this new technology were really just a *hypothesis*.

> **Standard deviation** (As a reminder) A measure of the variation of values from the mean (average), the average difference between any value in a set of values and the mean of all of the values in that set.

Do you remember back in grade school during the science fair events when you had to create a hypothesis? After creating the hypothesis, you then needed to test it by collecting data and experimenting to draw a conclusion and comparing it with your hypothesis. Just because you are in business now instead of school, that doesn't mean that you get to ignore the basic logic of what you learned in grade school! *It works!*

This was a company of 37 long-time employees and total revenues of $12 million. A wrong decision of this type could kill the company.

I was hired specifically to improve the current processes, but I felt obligated to stop the remaining half of the $4.7 million expenditure. The installation of the equipment was under way. I told the president that this method was not proven and I requested that he ask the following question of the supplier: "Where is the data that proves the hypothesis of the labor cost?" The president would not challenge or question the supplier. I then wrote a letter to the company management, advising that the decision to move forward was wrong and I would be disengaging from any further consulting activity. I fired the client! I am passionate about the well-being of my clients and, based on my six sigma expertise, I knew what the outcome for this company would be.

Before I left, I was able to complete a comparison of the new technology and the old method. The Analyze phase is all about making comparisons. Figure 8-1 is the graph of comparison.

If you look at this graph what would you conclude? I don't see much difference in the scatter of points. Do you?

As a matter of fact, the old method cost on average $519.57 per part and the new method cost on average $533.62 per part. There was *no* significant or practical difference in the methods—and the new method would cost more per part.

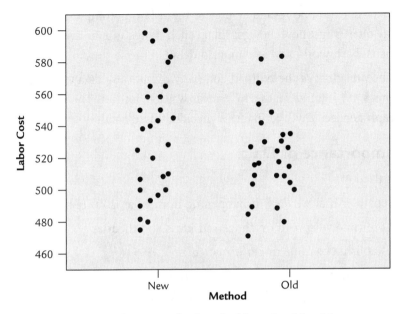

Figure 8-1. Costs of new method and old method for 30 parts

In this case, there was no data suggesting that the new equipment made a difference—or, in other words, there was no difference between old and new. The performance of the technology did not meet the stated criterion: it did not reduce labor, rework, and finishing quality by more than half.

This graph shows an autopsy of a wrong decision. The cost of not comparing for this company was death! The contract did not have performance clauses and the ego of the president would not yield. The practical difference between the old technology and the new technology was the *money* lost—$4.7 million! I now refer to this graph as the "$4.7-million death graph"!

Small businesses and start-ups don't have the time to do it over. The old saying, "We never have the time to do it right, but we always have time to do it over," is wrong! Small business leaders cannot be analytically detached experts. You don't have the funds to subsidize the wrong decision. The small business owner answers the phone, drives the truck, cleans the floor, whatever it takes; everyone obviously produces and contributes to bottom-line results or they're fired! But as companies get bigger, they often forget how they got there: such things as team involvement, consensus, hard work, and attention to detail.

The president of the railroad company did not use data to make his decisions and his father's father's business was lost forever! There was only one graph needed. *Don't* be like this president! Use data!

The Importance of Data

Data is used to:

- Separate what we *think* is happening from what is *really* happening
- Confirm or disprove preconceived ideas and theories
- Establish a baseline of performance
- See the history of the problem over time
- Measure the impact of changes on a process
- Identify and understand relationships that might help explain variation
- Control a process (monitor process performance)
- Avoid "solutions" that don't solve the real problem

In the Analyze phase we determine which X's are causing the problems in your critical metrics. When you *analyze* the data collected during the Measure phase, it is important to estimate the limits within which we can be confident that the small group sample statistics like mean and standard deviation are really telling us about differences in the total population. Hypothesis testing (comparisons) is the Analyze phase tool that leads us to the vital few variables. It's about comparing stuff!

Remember in Chapter 2 about opening the *Yellow Pages* for your city or town and finding thousands of small businesses with hundreds of thousands of defects. To get you into the frame of mind for the Analyze phase, bounce some questions against those defects that were pointed out in that chapter:

- **Accountants**—Have you ever had your income tax prepared incorrectly resulting in penalties? The hypothesis to ask is "Are all accountants the same?" You could compare the penalties or the number of incorrectly prepared tax returns.

- **Advertising and Media**—Have you ever spent too much for advertising without any return on your investment? Don't you wish you could get that money back? The hypothesis to ask is "Are all advertising and media companies the same?" You could compare their ROIs for each client.

- **Automobiles**—Have you ever had a dissatisfying experience with a local car dealership? The same hypothesis can be asked: "Are all dealerships the same?" In this industry your goal is to minimize your damage on price, repair, warranty, service time, etc.

You get the idea: there are defects everywhere and so many hypothesis questions to ask! The goal of asking hypothesis questions is to get to a new set of questions to find the solutions to the problems. The amount of money that can be saved with knowing the key factors driving the defect is between 15 percent and 25 percent of your total sales. The key question to constantly and relentlessly ask is: What are those defects a function of?

The Case of the Wasted Marketing Dollars

A small company had a theory that spending more on advertising would improve sales. Before I get into the specifics, let's look at the graph of the results (Figure 8-2).

What do you conclude from this graph? This is a company that was stuck in its advertising spending habits without any knowledge as to how it affected the company's sales. "It's the way we have always done our advertising and we believe that it works," stated the VP of sales. *Why?*

As a consultant to many small, medium, and large companies, I recognize that these words are the classic "It's the way we have always done it." Six Sigma is not about what you feel, think, or believe. It's not that we don't trust you; it's just that we want to see the data. The question to ask the VP of sales is "Can you show the data to support your belief?" The graph shows that any spending above $50,000 is a waste of money and also shows the company has wasted more than $125,000 on advertising that is ineffective because sales have not increased.

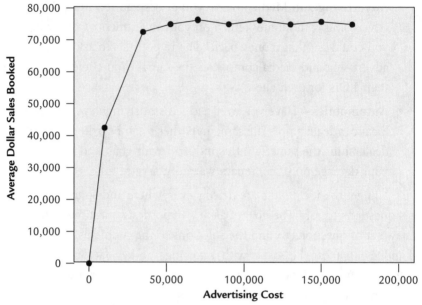

Figure 8-2. Cost advertising versus average dollars booked (sold)

Knowing that $Y = f(X)$, here are two questions to think about:

• To get results, should we focus our efforts on the Y or the X's ?

• If we are so good at X, why do we constantly test and inspect Y?

The Analyze phase is the testing phase for your questions on the X's. The Analyze phase helps us to determine what is vital and what is trivial. We'll show these tests as graphical methods to compare or graphical hypothesis to demonstrate the concept.

Overview of the Analyze Phase

Here are the basics to performing the Analyze phase, using graphical comparisons and hypotheses:

Begin with the Basics

There are major statistical tools in the Analyze phase. I don't want to trivialize these tools, but graphical methods are extremely powerful. The goal of this chapter is not to make you a Six Sigma power tool user, but to gain your respect for the basics that small businesses can use with little or no effort.

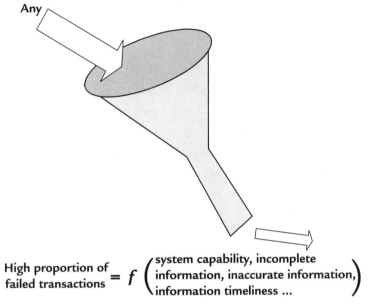

$$\text{High proportion of failed transactions} = f \left(\begin{array}{l} \text{system capability, incomplete} \\ \text{information, inaccurate information,} \\ \text{information timeliness ...} \end{array} \right)$$

Figure 8-3. Separating the trivial many from the vital few

1. Localize the problem.
2. State the relationship you are trying to establish.
3. Establish the hypothesis or the questions describing the problem.
4. Decide on appropriate techniques to prove your hypothesis.
5. Test the hypothesis using the data you collected in the Measure phase.
6. Analyze the results and reach conclusions.
7. Validate the hypothesis.

Step 1: Localize the Problem

To "localize" something means pinpoint where and when it appears and it doesn't appear. The basic question to ask is "Given all the possible X's that could be causing the Y to be a defect, which one or ones is or are the problem?" You are converting your thinking, believing, and feeling into a confidence or risk of being right or wrong. In the advertising story, the question should have been "Are we getting any more sales for our spending dollar on advertising?" This sets up the problem.

There are two major categories of problems that we are going to cover here.

The first one is when the mean (average) of the Y is off center from the desired specification. This is called a *mean center problem.*

Think about the normal distribution of data you'd get from a process. A mean center problem means that the center of that distribution curve is not at the center point between the specification limits, your target. In the football analogy, you'd see the football sailing over one side of the crossbar rather than through the center (Figure 8-4).

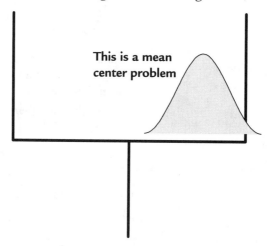

Figure 8-4. Mean center problem

The second type of problem is a *variance problem.* This is a widespread dispersion of the data. Variance problems reflect the range of experiences that your customers may have with your product or service. For example, one day they have to wait on hold for two minutes and the next day the phone is picked up on the first ring, or one widget they pick up has perfect dimensions, but the next one is a smidge too small or too wide. For the example of the kicker, a variance problem would be that the kicks spread out between and beyond the desired specification (Figure 8-5).

A problem can be a combination of both types, centering (mean center) problems that exhibit spread (variance) problems. The goal is to

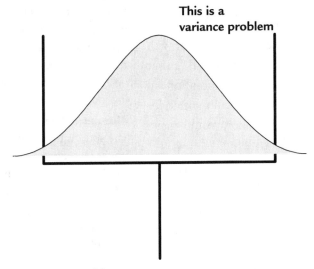

Figure 8-5. Variance problem

understand the problem in terms of mean or standard deviation, which helps define the type of problem you are trying to solve. This helps you use the proper methods to solve the problem.

Step 2: State the Relationship You Are Trying to Establish

The goal is to know how the Y that you want to achieve is connected to the X's that you're investigating. You're going to test for movement in a given Y (such as sales) in terms of the X's (such as advertising cost) you are investigating to prove your hypothesis. Advertising sales could also be a function of other X's, such as type of media, billboards, mail campaigns, lists of qualified prospects, promotions, web site techniques, PR, cold calling, buyer incentive programs, proper value proposition, pricing, availability, new VP of sales, etc.

Step 3: Establish the Hypothesis

When we establish a hypothesis, it's convention to state both a *null hypothesis* and an *alternative hypothesis*.

First, state the null hypothesis (H_o). This is the question of no difference. At the end of the test (either with graphics or statistics), you'll either accept the null (no differences) or fail to accept (that's statistician-speak for "reject") the null, which would mean there was a difference.

Then, state the alternative hypothesis (H_a). This is nothing more than the opposite of the null. If there are no differences, the alternative is that there are differences. As with the null hypothesis, you either accept the alter-

> **Null hypothesis (H_o)** The supposition that there is no difference between the groups you're comparing, that the factor under investigation is not making a difference.
>
> **Alternative hypothesis (H_a)** The supposition that the factor under investigation is making a difference, such that there is a difference between a group where the factor was present and a group where it was not present.

native (differences) or fail to accept (reject) the alternative (no difference).

Step 4: Decide on Appropriate Techniques to Test the Hypothesis

There are many high-powered statistical methods for testing hypotheses, but the goal is to present the concept of making comparisons, not to make you a Black Belt or bore you with statistics.

There is a basic graphical hypothesis technique that you can use to test your hypothesis. If the process is repetitive (more than three times a day), we can use this simple method to investigate the X's in question. All you need is a calculator, a pencil, and a blank sheet of paper.

Here's our scenario. A company just hired a new salesperson and sales rose for the next two months. The president checked on the new salesperson's performance one day (observed one data point of a major sale) and assumed that was how all the days went for that person—so he believed that the new person was the reason for the increase in sales.

To test this hypothesis, the president looked at the numbers for the new salesperson and one of the other top sales staff (Figure 8-6).

By the way, what the president observed was the new person's tenth

Day	New Salesperson	Top Salesperson
4	5,600	23,980
5	3,500	16,700
6	6,700	26,500
7	8,300	12,000
8	5,000	15,000
9	9,500	23,000
10	28,000	26,000
11	2,000	14,200
12	1,500	14,700
13	7,800	23,500
14	2,300	21,450
15	2,100	21,000
16	13,000	17,000
17	9,800	13,000
18	3,450	18,900

Figure 8-6. Sales: new salesperson and top salesperson

day and he assumed that all other days were the same. He didn't know that his top salesperson had given the new employee one of the large accounts to demonstrate a sales technique.)

Step 5: Test the Hypothesis Using the Data Collected in the Measure Phase

To test the null hypothesis that there is no difference between these two people vs. the alternative hypothesis that there is a difference, the president needed to calculate four things:

1. Mean
2. Standard deviation

Means Are Not Enough

Do not take the average number given to you as gospel. Why? Because you need to know what made up the average. You need to see the distribution of the data. Remember the histogram.

For example, web site statistics show that the average duration of a visit on your secondary page was 6.43 minutes for 1,200 hits. However, if you had only that mean and not the detailed raw data, you would not know that one visitor from 11:30 p.m. to 9:00 a.m. forgot to log off your web site, a single event that caused the mean duration to increase from ten seconds to 6.43 minutes. *Get the raw data!*

3. Average plus one standard deviation

4. Average minus one standard deviation

Figure 8-7 shows the calculations that the president did for the two salespeople. (He used a spreadsheet—a good idea if you're not comfortable with math or you want to crunch a lot of numbers fast. Most spreadsheets can calculate standard deviation.) He did not count the three days that were the first for the new salesperson, to allow him to acclimate.

Salesperson	Mean	Standard Deviation	(−1)Standard Deviation	(+1)Standard Deviation
New	7,327	6,681	646	14,008
Top	19,129	4,839	14,290	23,968

Figure 8-7. Calculations from the sales data

Step 6: Analyze the Results and Reach Conclusions

In this step, we determine whether or not we find true differences in the process with and without the factor that we hypothesized as being important. One way to do this is by using graphical tools.

Let's make a graph that compares the new salesperson and the top salesperson (Figure 8-8). The Y-axis is the sales and the X-axis is the two salespeople. The mean and standard deviation numbers show this new salesperson is not as good as the top salesperson.

The interpretation of the graph in Figure 8-6 is straightforward. It is similar to a stock chart showing the high, low, and close, only in this case you see the average (center point), +1 standard deviation (above), and −1 standard deviation (below).

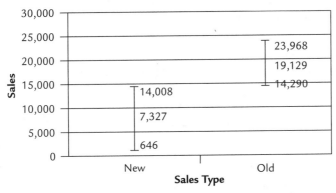

Figure 8-8. Comparison of new salesperson and top salesperson

If there is a gap anywhere between the lines of one group end and the lines of the other group start, you are likely to have a statistical difference. This is not mathematically correct, but it can be used as a basic guideline to testing for a statistical difference.

Step 7: Validate the Hypothesis

In statistical terms, graphs like these support your *confidence* in the conclusion that any observed differences are real or not (that is, whether they will persist over time). Before seeing this data, the president may have stated he was highly confident that the new salesperson was different from the top salesperson. Now he can say that with confidence, though not in the way he originally thought! He is now beyond "I think," "I feel," or "I believe" that the two salespeople are different.

The practical significance of this graph (what it does for the business) is that it shows that the new salesperson is OK, but not a paragon. Rather, the company would be much better off using the top salesperson as an on-the-job trainer for the rest of the salespeople. The president didn't need another salesperson; he needed to help the others improve!

Check the Distribution

Technically speaking, the hypothesis tests illustrated here work only if the data are distributed normally. (That's the bell-shaped curve that's referenced all the time.) A simple guideline to check the normality of the data is to use three standard deviations as the spread on each side of the mean. If most of the data falls within this spread, it is more than likely normal. If the data does not fit, then it is more than likely not normal: there are major variances or one-time events that are causing the mean to be distorted. In that case, ask a Master Black Belt or statistician for help!

Step 8: Conduct a Phase-Gate Review

At the end of the Analyze phase, just as in the Define and Measure phases, the Black Belt should report to the executive leaders on the status of the project. This presentation is an opportunity for you to ask questions, make suggestions, address any problems, allocate additional resources, provide support, and show your commitment. The phase-gate review also ensures that the team stays focused and the project stays on track.

Conclusion

In the Analyze phase you determine which X's are causing the problems in your critical metrics and come up with solutions targeted at the confirmed causes. In some cases you will be creating solutions with the tools you learned about in this chapter. However, you are now using data-driven decisions to make them. It is hard to argue with facts and data. The graphical hypothesis test, which is just making comparisons, is the major tool of the Analyze phase, in which we start funneling the X's that are vital factors.

Summary of the Major Steps in the Analyze Phase

1. Localize the problem.
2. State the relationship you are trying to establish.
3. Establish the hypothesis or the questions describing the problem.

4. Decide on appropriate techniques to prove your hypothesis.

5. Test the hypothesis using the data you collected in the Measure phase.

6. Analyze the results and reach conclusions.

7. Validate the hypothesis.

8. Conduct a phase-gate review.

   You are now ready to enter the Improve phase.

Chapter 9

Your Six Sigma Project: The Improve Phase

Without continual growth and progress, such words as improvement, achievement, and success have no meaning.
—Benjamin Franklin

I am the president and founder of a small community bank (three branches and an administrative office). I started the company on willpower, passion, a lack of money, and a dream to help people in need. It turned into a pride-swallowing activity focused on the employees and *not* customers' needs. We were flat for three years and further growth was nowhere in sight. I felt extremely alone and confused.

One day, I realized that I had spent 70 percent of my time that week on internal problems. I had a staff of six VP-level professionals who had been with me for over four years. What the hell were they doing?

Has this ever happened to you? Have you ever felt this way? I was being mentored by a Six Sigma consultant focused on fixing problems regardless of what, who, and how. He showed me that experience is important, but more important was the experience of dealing with wrong judgment. In the Improve phase of Six Sigma, I learned that unfiltered data and facts were vital for making good judgments, a major part of the Improve phase.

I was getting information from my staff that conflicted with facts coming from Six Sigma activities. It was to the point where I wanted to fire all my employees. I never thought my staff members would be gremlins, but I was sick of the gremlin-like behavior that was going on—they were much more concerned about what was in this for them than what was important to customers.

Then my mentor told me that I was the root of the problem, because I allowed this to happen! He then conducted an activity-based time analysis on the bank to determine what management and key personnel were doing for growth. We had three strategy sessions to create a plan for growth, but it was not working.

We were determined to find a plan that would work. My mentor told me that it would be based on data and that I would have to make a judgment on the plan and implement it with the full support of my team. He was brutally direct with his concerns for the gremlins and told me to deal with these issues using data.

When we reached the Improve phase, he started his presentation with a quote:

> "In every revolution there is one man with a vision."
>   —Captain James T. Kirk

A thorough analysis of the commercial and retail banking issues showed that the breakthrough vital factors related to no cross-selling efforts on current accounts. We had a database of customer information showing commercial and retail checking accounts but no other products, such as loans or money markets. We had growth opportunity within our own accounts but there was no activity to sell our high-quality products and services to our customers. We were spending our time maintaining accounts, not growing them.

An additional surprise to me was that only 0.68 percent of the commercial accounts were using our construction loans, when about 12 percent needed construction loans. This was a minimum growth of $1.5 million. Our customers didn't know about our products. We knew about their wants and absolutely ignored them.

My team was in total disbelief and denial regarding the reality of the data presented by the Six Sigma consultant. I felt the goal of my team was to get rid of him and discredit me in his eyes.

I was at a crossroads. The Six Sigma mentor called it the "Six Sigma Judgment Day." The final tally was a conservative estimate of $13 million in growth that we were neglecting. I asked my mentor what he would do. He told me that the business was eroding internally and my next decision would determine how long it would survive. He strongly recommended I surround myself with people who were more concerned about the bank and less about their functional silos. To set the tone of importance for growing this business, he recommended I fire the commercial vice president for nonperformance. Also, using internal data, we should create a surgical marketing plan to send promotions to highly potential customers.

I realized that I had lost my edge as president of the company, but I regained it in the Six Sigma Improve phase, where the solutions became reality and I made a decision to improve. I rid myself of the VPs for Human Resources, Commercial, and Retail, and drove the improvements to completion. I promoted new leaders into these functions from within and the result was awesome. In six months we had 5 percent growth using the surgical plan from our Six Sigma consultant. A year later we had achieved $7 million in growth. And we were just getting started!

Every time I tell this story, I feel sorry for those leaders who lose their grip on what made them successful. This president was not getting the real story and was in an ivory tower, just like the emperor without any clothes. Change is part of business and keeping grounded in the reality of the business is a leadership requirement for doing Six Sigma. This bank president enabled this environment and, without Six Sigma, he would not have changed until it was too late. The main question for a small business owner is: Are you ready to improve? Be careful what you wish for!

The Improve Phase

You are now in the Improve phase. The project team is ready to test and implement solutions to improve the process.

The Improve phase comes naturally to all of us. The key to the

Improve phase is creating the relationship between the X's and the Y's that you are trying to improve.

Here are the questions for the Improve phase:

1. What is the possible root cause of defects?

2. How can you prevent or eliminate these causes?

3. What changes in product, service, or process design are required to achieve your improvement goals? How do you know those changes will be effective?

4. What are your next steps toward achieving your improvement targets?

5. Has Finance been involved in the project to fully understand the cost implications of your improvement plans?

6. Are you satisfied with the level of cooperation and support you are getting?

7. What other support actions or activities do you need to accelerate your progress?

Remember that the Improve phase is about good judgment and using data to derive solutions. I encourage you to come up with crazy radical ideas for solutions, but make sure you have the relationship of the Y's and X's (proof). Improving your ability to improve is one focus of the Improve phase.

Let's recap your project from the Measure phase. You know your key metrics and you know the data being collected is valid. The Analyze phase has created a set of qualified X's suspected of causing the defects.

There are many more topics that could be covered here, but the heart of the Improve phase is question 3 above: What changes are you going to make and how do you know that they will be effective? Two common techniques used to answer the second part of that question are *correlation analysis* and *experimentation* (more specifically a technique called *design of experiments*).

Correlation Analysis

In the Improve phase you are establishing the relationship between inputs and outputs: you're trying to figure out which X's are most affecting the Y's. The simple way of doing this is a graphical method of correlation.

Correlation analysis determines the extent to which values of two quantitative variables are proportional to each other and expresses it in terms of a *correlation coefficient*. *Proportional* means linearly related; that is, the correlation is high if it can be approximated by a straight line (sloped upwards or downwards). Correlation measures the degree of linearity between two variables.

The value of the correlation coefficient is independent of the specific measurement units used; for example, the correlation between height and weight will be identical whether measured in inches and pounds or in centimeters and kilograms.

Correlation lies between -1 and +1. As a general rule, a correlation higher than .80 is important and a correlation lower than .20 is not significant. However, be careful with sample size. (We'll discuss the importance of sample size a little later.)

> **Correlation** Degree to which two variables are related, which is measured by a *correlation coefficient*, a number between +1 (positive linear correlation) and –1 (negative linear correlation), with 0 indicating no linear correlation

The coefficient of linear correlation "r" is the measure of the strength of the correlation. (Known as Pearson r, this is the most widely used type of correlation coefficient; it's also called *linear correlation* or *product-moment correlation.*)

The typical correlation patterns are depicted in the scatter plots in Figure 9-1. A downward sloping line indicates negative correlation and an upward sloping line indicates positive correlation no correlation, with the degree of slope corresponding to the strength of either type of correlation.

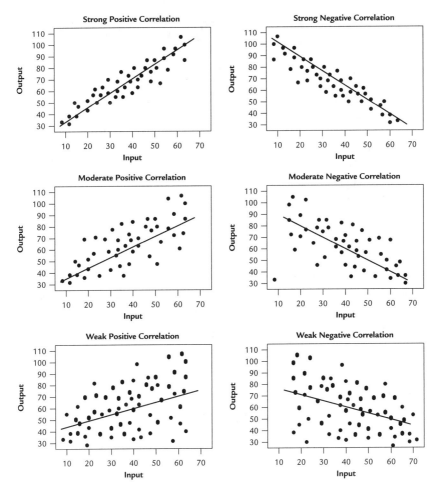

Figure 9-1. Typical correlation patterns

OK, so how does all of that work and how does it help us? To discuss correlation analysis, let's use the scatter plot shown in Chapter 8, the graph depicting the relationship between advertising expenditures and sales (Figure 9-2). Is there a relationship between advertising cost and average sales dollars booked?

Figure 9-3 shows a simple graphical method to estimate the correlation coefficient (r) for your scatter plot data.

These are the steps to determine r correlation.

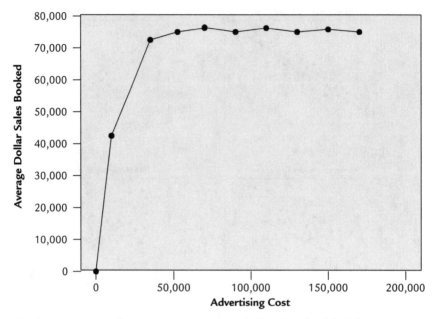

Figure 9-2. Cost advertising vs. average dollars booked (sold)

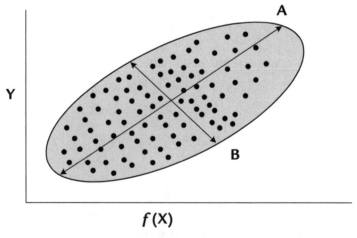

Figure 9-3. Graphical method for determining correlation

1. Draw an oval around the plot of points.

2. Measure the *maximum* diameter (A) of the oval with a scale.

3. Measure the *minimum* diameter (B) of the oval with a scale.

4. The value of r is estimated by ±(1-(B/A)), where the sign is a plus if the A diameter slopes upward and minus if the A diameter slopes downward.

Apply the Pareto Principle

Here are some guidelines for drawing the oval around data points for the graphical method of r correlation analysis:

1. The target is to ensure that the oval encompasses 80 percent of the data points.
2. No more than three data points can be outside the lower half of the oval.
3. No more than three data points can be outside the upper half of the oval.

Now let's answer the question about the scatter plot showing advertising expenditures and sales (Figure 9-4). Is there a correlation?

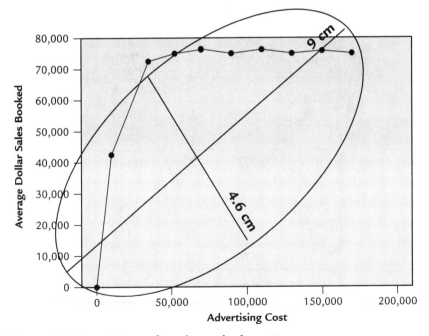

Figure 9-4. Correlation r for sales and advertising

We draw an oval around the plot of points on the printed graph. We measure the maximum diameter (A) and the minimum diameter (B): A is 9 cm and B is 4.6 cm. (The measurement units are not important so long as they are the same.) We use the formula $\pm(1-(B/A))$: $1 - (4.6/9) = 0.48$. Since diameter A slopes upward, we use a plus sign for our coefficient r: +0.48.

Can we infer from our coefficient that there is some correlation between our two variables? To answer that question, we use *decision points*. We find our coefficient in a decision points table (Figure 9-5). (If the coefficient is negative, we disregard the minus sign when we use this table.) The table sets decision points according to the sample size—the number of sample sets of Y and X (expressed as n). Those points determine the strength of the correlation.

If our coefficient is less than or equal to the decision point for our sample size, then we cannot say whether or not there is any correlation between our two variables. If our correlation is greater than the decision point, then there is some correlation. If our coefficient is positive, the correlation is positive; if our coefficient is negative, the correlation is negative.

n	Decision Point	n	Decision Point
5	0.878	18	0.468
6	0.811	19	0.456
7	0.754	20	0.444
8	0.707	22	0.423
9	0.666	24	0.404
10	0.632	26	0.388
11	0.602	28	0.374
12	0.576	30	0.361
13	0.553	40	0.312
14	0.532	50	0.279
15	0.514	60	0.254
16	0.497	80	0.220
17	0.482	100	0.196

Figure 9-5. Sample size (n) and decision point

Our sample size is 10, so the decision point (Figure 9-5) is 0.632, which puts it toward the positive end of the scale (Figure 9-6). Our correlation coefficient r is 0.48, which is below the decision point.

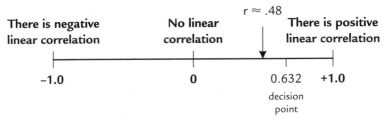

Figure 9-6. Correlation interpretation using decision point

This simply means there is no correlation between advertising dollars and sales dollars. In other words, you don't know the relationship between advertising and sales, so you are spending money on unknown assumptions and making business decisions that are no better than a WAG (wild-ass guess). Or maybe you're fooling yourself into thinking you're using a SWAG (scientific wild-ass guess)!

Of course, we already knew from Chapter 8 that the graph shows that any spending above $50,000 is a waste of money because beyond that point sales have not increased. So, why do we need correlation analysis when common sense shows what we need to know, that we should stop spending money when we're not getting any return on our dollars?

This is only a simple example, so you understand how to use correlation analysis for more difficult situations. Here's another example, one for which common sense would not be enough.

A small home healthcare business wants to add three locations. However, the owner doesn't know what nearby locations offer the greatest opportunity. He had an idea that the key factor for opportunity can be proportional to the number of people 65 or older in key locations.

He did some research to test this hypothesis of a relationship between the 65-plus population and the number of patients requiring home healthcare. The table in Figure 9-7 shows the data he collected.

He graphed the data points, drew an oval around them (excluding three data points above and one below and including 15 of 19 points, 79 percent), and measured the two diameters of the oval (Figure 9-8).

Data Point	Medicare Patients	People Over 65
1	2,936	20,071
2	3,748	13,345
3	3,385	22,253
4	3,740	31,770
5	3,314	27,994
6	3,646	27,920
7	3,810	39,856
8	4,476	31,050
9	2,231	11,092
10	1,302	6,141
11	4,354	24,058
12	1,779	7,157
13	2,510	14,076
14	2,795	16,392
15	2,258	10,685
16	1,726	4,935
17	2,072	5,699
18	1,626	7,520
19	2,239	6,405

Figure 9-7. Data for Medicare patients and people over 65

He then calculated the r correlation using $\pm 1 - (B/A)$: $1 - (1.5/6) =$ .75. The decision point in Figure 9-5 for a sample size of 19 is 0.456. Since r is greater than the decision point, there's a positive correlation.

We can conclude that the owner of the home healthcare business can use the relationship between the number of people older than 65 and the number of Medicare patients—potential customers for his home healthcare service—in making decisions about expanding his business. See the sidebar on the page 153 for a caution on the use of correlation.

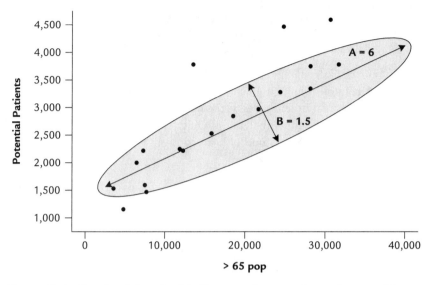

Figure 9-8. Graph of data for Medicare patients and people over 65

Design of Experiments

As I mentioned earlier in this chapter, in the Improve phase we must determine what changes we're going to make and how we can know that they will be effective. We've discussed one way, correlation analysis. The second common approach is experimentation.

An experiment is any testing in which the inputs are either controlled or directly manipulated according to a plan. We're trying to figure out what X's in our process have the greatest effect on the Y's that are our CTQs.

In the last chapter I mentioned grade school science fair projects. The traditional way to do those experiments is to evaluate only one variable at a time, keeping all of the other variables constant. That's simple. However, this approach has a major disadvantage: it does not show what would happen if two or more variable changed at the same time. We could run the experiment once for every possible combination of factors, to test all possible interactions among the factors, but that could mean running a lot of experiments; for example, if there are five factors, we would need to run the experiment 32 times.

Using Correlation Can Be Dangerous

In correlation analysis, we must keep in mind a basic truth: correlation does not imply causation. It can indicate the probability of a cause-and-effect relationship between two variables, but it's not proof.

Here's an example. The figure below shows variables for population and storks. The population increases as the number of storks increases. From this graph and correlation analysis, you might conclude that removing storks would be a good method of birth control!

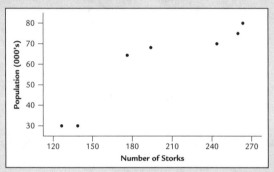

We may identify a relationship by observing a process and noting that two variables tend to increase together and decrease together. However, this does not mean that we can adjust one variable by manipulating the other variable. Correlation does *not* imply causation!

Adapted from: George E.P. Box, William G. Hunter, and J. Stuart Hunter, *Statistics for Experimenters*, p. 8

That's why we use design of experiments (DOE), a strategy for running tests according to a specific structure and with a specific methodology for analyzing the results. We determine settings for each of the input variables (factors) in advance. Then, during the experiment, we adjust the factors to the specified settings, run the process, and measure and record the output (response) variable for one or more units of output—transactions, products, or services delivered. We then analyze the data to determine the vital few input factors and we create a model to estimate $y = f(x)$.

Here we are going demonstrate the power of DOE using basic graphical techniques to show how the basics work. (You can find more details at www.isixsigma.com.)

Overview of the Improve Phase

Here are the basic steps in the Improve phase, using DOE:

1. Define the problem.
2. Establish the experimental objective.
3. Select the variables and choose the levels for the input variables.
4. Select the experimental design.
5. Run the experiment and collect data.
6. Analyze the data.
7. Draw practical conclusions.
8. Replicate or validate the experimental results.

Step 1: Define the Problem

You must describe the problem in practical business terms that all people familiar with the situation will understand in the same way. For example, an experiment is being run to evaluate the adverse cost impact that advertising, media, and sales force size have on seasonal profits. So, we might define the problem as follows: "Historical data indicates that spending is all over the map with no understanding of the return for the money spent, resulting in tripling the cost to our business." The problem should be defined in a way that is clear and practical to the company.

Step 2: Establish the Experimental Objective

The owners of the business desire to be more confident in their plan for seasonal promotional expenditures. They might set this objective: "The experiment should show that our plan will reduce cost by 70 percent with no adverse effects to seasonal customer requirements."

Step 3: Select the Variables and Choose the Levels for the Input Variables

Select both the output (response) variables—the Y's—and the input (independent) variables—the X's. Then, choose the levels for each input variable.

This is where we need to get a little technical. A *level* on a variable is simply a setting, a value. Generally, we set two levels—low or minimum and high or maximum. Sometimes we set a third—normal or mean.

For example, using data collected in the Measure or Analyze phases, you could pick the extremes of the process.

> **Keep It Simple**
>
> When choosing the input variables, keep it simple. Experience suggests there are generally only two to six "vital few" X's. Test the most likely first, of course. It is a judgment call—and sometimes you will have to select more.

For advertising expenditures, you could pick the cost figures from a low week and from a high week. For cashiers, you could set experience levels: less than three months' experience as low and experience greater than one year as high.

The levels represent the range of reality for each X. A machine can be dirty or clean, a cycle time can be long or short, a type of transaction can be simple or hard, or a discrete attribute can be yes or no, on or off, and so forth. You want to use values that will truly test the impact of each variable. The range must be wide enough to show a difference—not beyond the range of feasibility, but maybe beyond the current process range. Realize that some combinations in the test will produce unacceptable units: these results are expected and accepted. Some defects are the price to pay for understanding the process better.

We code the two levels as -1 (low) and +1 (high), to keep the records simple. For example, for advertising cost, $54,000 per month is −1 (low level) and $76,000 per month is +1 (high level).

Step 4: Select the Experimental Design

There are many DOE designs and complex methods. We will focus on the basic concepts. The experimental design is a simple table or matrix of possible combinations of factors and levels you are studying, a method of structuring and tracking the combinations.

A single combination is called a *treatment combination*. The level of the factors at a given condition is the treatment combination that results in a given observation that is recorded for later analysis.

Here is a basic experiment to which we all can relate: setting temperature for a shower. There are two variables: the hot water (105 degrees) and cold water (50 degrees). We will have two levels, extreme settings: low pressure when you move the knob a quarter turn counterclockwise (pressure at a factor of one) and high pressure when you move it two full turns counterclockwise (pressure at a factor of eight).

What are all the possible combinations? We have two factors and two levels for each. The experimental design for two factors at two levels can be calculated as 2^k where 2 is the number of levels for each factor and k is the number of factors. That gives us four treatment combinations (Figure 9-9).

Number	Cold Knob	Hot Knob	Desired Temperature
1	Low (−1)	Low (−1)	Observed
2	Low (−1)	High (+1)	Observed
3	High (+1)	Low (−1)	Observed
4	High (+1)	High (+1)	Observed

Figure 9-9. Design table: two factors (hot and cold), two levels (low and high)

Figure 9-10 shows the number of combinations for 2^k when we increase the number of factors.

k	Combinations	k	Combinations
3	8	6	64
4	16	7	128
5	32	8	256

Figure 9-10. Number of combinations of factors (2^k)

What happens if we have three factors? We would have eight combinations, as shown in the design table below (Figure 9-11).

Combination	Factor (X1)	Factor (X2)	Factor (X3)	Y
1	–1 (low)	–1 (low)	–1 (low)	Record
2	–1 (low)	–1 (low)	+1 (high)	Record
3	–1 (low)	+1 (high)	–1 (low)	Record
4	–1 (low)	+1 (high)	+1 (high)	Record
5	+1 (high)	–1 (low)	–1 (low)	Record
6	+1 (high)	–1 (low)	+1 (high)	Record
7	+1 (high)	+1 (high)	–1 (low)	Record
8	+1 (high)	+1 (high)	+1 (high)	Record

Figure 9-11. Design table: three factors, two levels

If we added a factor, we would have 16 combinations (Figure 9-12).

Step 5: Run the Experiment and Collect Data

You have designed the experiment. The design table or matrix is your plan for setting the factors to the levels specified in the treatment combinations. Now it is time to run the experiment and record the data.

To make sure that the results of our experiment are valid, we *replicate* the design: we run each treatment combination more than once.

Let's take our simple experiment for getting the desired temperature for the water. Figure 9-13 shows the results for three trials each of four treatment combinations of factors. Y1, Y2, and Y3 are the resulting temperature measurements.

Combination	Factor (X1)	Factor (X2)	Factor (X3)	Factor (X3)	Y
1	-1 (low)	-1 (low)	-1 (low)	-1 (low)	Record
2	-1 (low)	-1 (low)	+1 (high)	-1 (low)	Record
3	-1 (low)	+1 (high)	-1 (low)	-1 (low)	Record
4	-1 (low)	-1 (low)	+1 (high)	+1 (high)	Record
5	-1 (low)	+1 (high)	-1 (low)	-1 (low)	Record
6	-1 (low)	+1 (high)	-1 (low)	+1 (high)	Record
7	-1 (low)	+1 (high)	+1 (high)	-1 (low)	Record
8	-1 (low)	+1 (high)	+1 (high)	+1 (high)	Record
9	+1 (high)	-1 (low)	-1 (low)	-1 (low)	Record
10	+1 (high)	-1 (low)	-1 (low)	+1 (high)	Record
11	+1 (high)	-1 (low)	+1 (high)	-1 (low)	Record
12	+1 (high)	-1 (low)	+1 (high)	+1 (high)	Record
13	+1 (high)	+1 (high)	-1 (low)	-1 (low)	Record
14	-1 (low)	+1 (high)	+1 (high)	+1 (high)	Record
15	+1 (high)	+1 (high)	+1 (high)	-1 (low)	Record
16	+1 (high)	+1 (high)	+1 (high)	+1 (high)	Record

Figure 9-12. Design table: four factors, two levels

Combination	Cold Knob	Hot Knob	YI	Y2	Y3
1	Low (-1)	Low (-1)	84	81	83
2	Low (-1)	High (+1)	95	94	93
3	High (+1)	Low (-1)	71	70	72
4	High (+1)	High (+1)	84	81	82

Figure 9-13. Experiment results: temperatures measured for combinations

Step 6: Analyze the Data

There are many techniques for analyzing the results of DOE. Again our focus here is to demonstrate the power of DOE and to demonstrate the basic interpretation graphically.

The first graphical plot (Figure 9-14) can be of the individual data points and the output for each treatment combination. This is the individual value plot, which is used to assess and compare X's (inputs) and Y's (outputs) by plotting individual values for each variable or group in a vertical column, making it easy to spot trends.

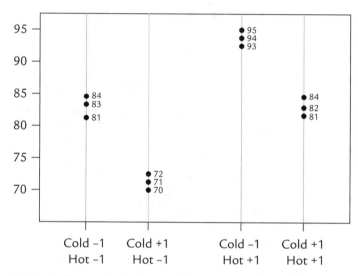

Figure 9-14. Indirect value plot: combinations and resulting temperatures

If you wanted the temperature was to be as hot as possible, you could visually see on the plot which settings you should use—hot on high and cold on low. The graph clearly demonstrates the settings and possible output ranges.

We could also plo the effect of cold and the effect of hot on separate charts. This could be a valuable graphic toold for more complex experiments. Here, however we can use Figure 9-14. To separate the effect of cold, we can compare the temperatures that result when cold is high (second and fourth columns) and the temperatures that result when cold is low (first and third columns). Likewise, to separate the effect of hot, we can compare the temperatures that result when hot is high (third and fourth columns) and the temperatures that result when hot is low (first and second columns).

> **Main effect** The simple effect of a factor on a dependent variable, measured as the average change in the output between the low and high levels of that factor for all the levels of the other factors, in contrast with *interaction effect*, an effect of two or more factors together.

Another extremely visual graphical plot is the *main effects plot*. (A main effect is the impact of a single input variable on the response variable.) We use the main effects plot for data means (averages) when we have multiple factors. It gives us the following information:

- It ranks the factors from most important to least important, not including the interactions.

- It indicates the best setting for each of the factors.

We plot the means of the response variable at each level of each factor. Then we draw a line to connect the high mean and the low mean for each factor. The flatter the reference line, the less effect that factor has on the response variable. The higher the slope of the reference line, the more that factor is affecting the response variable.

Setting	Combinations	Mean Temperature
Cold Low (−1)	1 and 2	84+81+83+95+94+93 = 88.33
Cold Low (+1)	3 and 4	71+70+72+84+81+82 = 76.66
Hot Low (−1)	1 and 3	84+81+83+71+70+72 = 76.83
Hot High (+1)	2 and 4	95+94+93+84+81+82 = 88.16

Figure 9-15. Mean values for results for all settings

First we need to calculate the average of the three results—Y1, Y2, and Y3—for each factor at each level, as shown in Figure 9-14.

Then we plot those mean temperatures on a main effects plot (Figure 9-16).

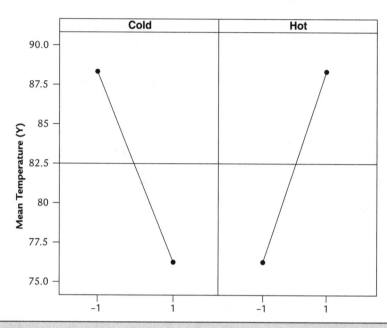

Don't Assume

In reality you cannot assume that all systems are alike. When I first ran the cold and hot experiment, the results didn't seem logical: hot had a greater effect than cold. To make sense of those results, I investigated and found that the pressure was being restricted by a valve hidden behind the wall. I then equalized the pressure on both knobs.

We refer to this hidden factor as a *lurking variable* because it is lurking behind the factors. It typically takes a closer examination of the problem to uncover this factor. Don't assume!

Step 7: Draw Practical Conclusions

There is a dilemma in this very important step. You could have a major practical significance from your DOE, but have no statistical significance. *I want you to know the difference—it will make the difference between success and failure.*

For example, you make a product with a recipe that uses six ingredients. You use DOE and find that you can decrease significantly the amount of one of the ingredients and any difference in the quality of the recipe is of no *statistical* significance. The pure statistician who does not know your business will not know the *practical* significance of that finding. So, if the cake tastes the same with or without the ingredient, why bother with removing it? But you know that the difference of no statistical significance has a practical significance: that one ingredient accounts for 40 percent of the total cost, which you could cut in half without affecting the quality of the recipe.

You need to know both the practical and statistical significance of your conclusions.

Here's another example. A call center added 15 operators to reduce hold time. That change resulted in a *statistically* significant difference in hold time, but the cost of adding the operators didn't make the reduction in hold time *practically* significant in terms of the adverse effect on the profit margin. The call center eventually had to lay off those new hires, which resulted in two employee-related lawsuits.

Step 8: Replicate or Validate the Experimental Results

Make sure to validate your DOE conclusions by running your desired settings. The validation will be self-evident when the results are what you concluded.

Implement the solutions, *get the money, improve, and create a phenomenal customer experience!*

Step 9: Conduct a Phase-Gate Review

At the end of the Improve phase, just as in the earlier phases, the Black Belt should report to the executive leaders on the status of the project. This presentation is an opportunity for you to ask questions, make suggestions, address any problems, allocate additional resources, provide support, and show your commitment. The phase-gate review at this, like the other stages, continues to ensure that the team stays focused and the project stays on track.

Conclusion

You are now ready to enter the final phase of Six Sigma: Control. In the Improve phase you have established the relationship between the Y's and the X's that is causing the problems in your critical metrics. In some cases, you will be creating solutions with the tools you learned about in this chapter. Your good judgment and data-driven decisions will make those solutions a success. The DOE and correlation analysis graphical methods, as presented in this chapter, require little mathematical know-how but provide statistically correct results. The graphical demonstrations clearly show the power of the tools.

The goal of DOE is to cause an informative event that can be observed. The experiments actively manipulate independent variables (input) and show the effects on dependent variables (output). Through experimental design we can demonstrate the ability to manipulate (or control) the output variables by making changes to the input variables. But we must always remember to make a *practical* conclusion as well as a *statistical* conclusion.

Summary of the Major Steps in the Improve Phase

1. Define the problem.
2. Establish the experimental objective.
3. Select the variable and choose the levels for the input variables.
4. Select the experimental design.
5. Run the experiment and collect data.
6. Analyze the data.
7. Draw practical conclusions.
8. Replicate or validate the experimental results.
9. Conduct a Phase-Gate Review

Improving your ability to improve is the focus of the Improve phase! Now we have to control our process!

6σ SB | # Chapter 10
Your Six Sigma Project: The Control Phase

Never be afraid to do something new. Remember:
amateurs built the ark; professionals built the Titanic.
—Unknown

"See if you agree with me on this common problem. I have a small printing business and employee errors are driving me crazy. One customer rejection or one shipping error can cost me a customer and a month's profit. I've fired people. I've yelled and screamed. I've trained till I'm blue in the face, and still I have errors. I know large companies talk about 'zero defects,' but is that possible? Are my expectations unrealistic? I sometimes want to give up!"

I met Tom Meeker on a flight from New York on my way home from visiting one of my clients. I agreed that employees were making errors, but did not agree on his approach to fixing the problem. I decided to help him understand that there is no such thing as intentionally bad employees or employees going to work to make errors intentionally. I started with the Define and Measure phases to understand his key metrics.

I told Tom that his process allowed or even promoted many employee errors. His process had no checkpoints, no measurements to verify possible errors, and no performance standards indicating trends.

Tom's main measurement was complaint calls from customers who were "firing" his company for errors.

The first thing you must do is recognize your part in the problem and take responsibility. Tom did not like what I had to say, but he could not prove to himself or me that the problem really was those so-called "dumb employees." My hidden agenda is to stop employers from blaming innocent employees. I have seen many large plants and businesses in rural America doing massive layoffs that they could have avoided by using Six Sigma. It's sickening to watch the devastation that does not have to occur!

I proceeded to push Tom on the process issues, and we examined an example of a customer rejection. We did a hypothetical review using Define, Measure, Analyze, Improve, and Control. Tom's epiphany finally came in the Control phase. When customers rejected orders, it was typically because the binding they received was not what they'd requested. I recommended a control method called *mistake proofing*. This ensured that the mistake was stopped at the source.

In this case, mistake proofing involved changing the software. The order form the employees used was on the computer. They marked choices on the order form by circling the items. But the choice of binding had to be written in instead of circled. That part of the order form caused variation among order takers. The five choices should have been listed on the form.

Tom felt embarrassed by the simplicity of this prevention measure and completely humiliated during our discussion. I reassured him that his feelings were typical and showed that he was learning to take responsibility for his actions. In the end he thanked me for my candid feedback. Two weeks later Tom e-mailed me the results of some initial changes he had made. They had stopped the binding error and initiated several more changes in his business processes. This is one of hundreds of stories that are constantly in my life. Please take it to heart for your business.

The Control Phase

You and your team have gone through the initial four phases of the Six Sigma DMAIC model. You've picked a project, measured the current state of the project, identified the vital few X's that cause the defects, and established the relationship for the CTQ or Y of the project and the vital few X's. Now you are ready to *control* the X's to ensure a sustained predictable Y. That is the sole purpose of the Control phase.

The main methods used in the Control phase are statistical process control (SPC) and mistake proofing. These methods complete the cycle of finding the controls for the solution and, more importantly, maintaining the control of the solution. You cannot assume that training or changing policies or procedures will be adequate to achieve control. You must ask the right questions to ensure control. Here are some of those questions:

> **How to Avoid the Control Phase**
>
> You cannot skip or get around the Control phase unless you eliminate the defect. There are many situations in which a Six Sigma team finds that no control is necessary because the team made the cause of the defect completely go away by setting and maintaining the right inputs.

1. What is your plan to enforce policy and procedures?

2. What chart will be used to show how the process is working and ensure control of the solution?

3. Who is responsible for maintaining the solutions and control plans?

4. What are the consequences when the process is out of control?

5. What is the communication or training plan to sustain control?

6. Who will document and implement the monitoring plan?

7. What will be the standardized process?

8. What is the plan to share the knowledge gained on the process so it is institutionalized?

9. What is the review plan to maintain the gain?

The Control phase ensures the new process conditions are documented and monitored via process control methods. After a settling-in period, the process capability should be reassessed. Depending upon the outcomes of such a follow-on analysis, it may be necessary to revisit one or more of the preceding phases.

We'll emphasize SPC (statistical process control) and cover the simple methods only.

Statistical Process Control (SPC)

SPC (statistical process control) was developed by Walter Shewhart in 1924. SPC is a statistically based graphing technique that compares current process data with a set of stable control limits established from normal process variation. When data points go beyond those control limits or when certain patterns appear between the limits, a process is said to be *out of control* (meaning out of *statistical* control).

As mentioned before, the Six Sigma approach often says that *Y is a function of X*, in short, $Y = f(X)$, to represent the idea that any output is a function of some input factors (X's) and that some of these X's are the vital few variables.

If we collected data only pertaining to the outcome (Y) in the Control phase, then we would be practicing statistical process *monitoring*, an approach that is *reactive* and doesn't allow us to control the process. We collect data on the X's, an approach that is *proactive*—that's what makes it statistical process *control*. The focus of control must be on drivers—X's that are directly related to the Y's.

A natural question is "Do we need statistical process control if we have already identified the vital few variables and if we made the process healthy in the Improve phase? In the ideal world, the outcome of the Improve phase is a healthy process resulting in a yield that is close to six sigma levels. In such cases, monitoring or controlling the process would not be required. But we know not everything in life works according to plan, so we implement control and monitoring tools to help us ensure that the processes remain close to six sigma levels. In other words, we sustain the gains.

There are many benefits to using statistical process control.

- (SPC) groups data into patterns that can be statistically tested, and provides insight about the behavior of products or process characteristics.

- SPC facilitates the understanding of the underlying cause system of products and process characteristics.

- SPC provides a graphical representation of product or process performance.

- SPC detects *assignable causes* that affect the central tendency, and/or the variability of the sources from variation and defects.

The main use of SPC is that it serves as a decision making tool based on probabilities, acts as a practical tool for detecting changes in product and/or process performance in relation

> **Central tendency** Where the data points cluster (which is at the average or mean in normally distributed data).

to historical performance, or specified standards, allows decisions (inferences) to be made based on sample data and points out when action is needed with known levels of risk and confidence.

Overview of the Control Phase

Here are the basic steps in the Control phase, using the standard steps for SPC, to serve as a guideline for working with control charts:

1. Select the variable to chart.
2. Select the type of control chart to use.
3. Determine rational subgroup size and sampling interval/frequency.
4. Determine measurement methods and criteria.
5. Calculate the parameters of the control chart.
6. Develop a control plan.
7. Train the people and use the charts.
8. Conduct a phase-gate review.

Step 1: Select the Variable to Chart

The input variable that you'll be charting ideally should be critical. Which input variable did design of experiments show to be most important in its impact on the critical output variable?

What types of values do you have for your X? What type of data will you be collecting? Remember that there are two types of data:

- Attribute data is discrete (either-or) data, such as yes or no, clean or dirty, high or low, 0 or 1, etc.
- Variable data is data measured on a continuous scale, such as pressure, weight, dimensions, cycle time, time, or temperature.

The type of data that you'll be collecting will determine in part the type of control charts you'll be using.

It is possible to convert from attribute to variable, in order to get specific with the root of a problem. When you use variable data, you do not need as much, since it provides a distribution, not just an either-or. To convert from discrete data to variable, you break down the breakpoint, if possible: work with the reasoning behind the either-or to create a scale. For example, for roofs, if the attribute is flatness (flat or not flat), you would use the determinant for that decision, degree of slope, as the scale. Or for transactions, if the attribute is good or bad, the criterion for that judgment, such as cost per transaction or cycle time of the transaction, could be used as the scale.

Step 2: Select the Type of Control Chart to Use

The rules for calculating control limits vary according to the type of data you have, so you should select the chart according to the type of data you'll be collecting and sample size, as shown in Figure 10-1.

At this point, you can only narrow down the choice of charts according to your type of data. For variable data, you would use Xi, X-bar and R, and X-bar and sigma charts. For attribute data, you would use C, U, NP, or P charts. Then, to determine the chart, you move on to deciding on sampling. We'll discuss these control charts in step 5.

Step 3: Determine Rational Subgroup Size and Sampling Interval/Frequency

How much data do you collect? How often do you collect data? Both size and frequency matter greatly.

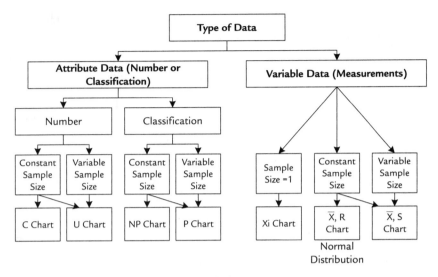

Figure 10-1. Data types and control charts

The rational subgroup is the basis of control charts. You cannot do random sampling. You must sample rationally, by sampling groups of items that came through the process under the same conditions. You will calculate and plot the statistics for each subgroup separately.

Rational subgrouping is a method for determining the size and frequency of sampling so that each sample accurately represents a point in time or space. We've all heard that it's not smart to buy a car that was built on a Monday or a Friday because the workers aren't doing their best on those days. If the factory were collecting data using a subdivision of the days of the week over certain hours of the day, you would know what was happening from the entire process by rationing where and when you get the data.

> **Rational subgrouping** A method for determining the size and frequency of sampling so that each sample accurately represents a point in time or space.

Rational subgrouping is the way to collect data that best represents a process state that is unknown. But it must be done carefully. Improper rational subgrouping can lead to the inclusion of special-cause effects in the variation within a subgroup. It can also result in missing the non-random variation among the subgroups. As a consequence, you might get a wrong perception of the situation and thus act inappropriately.

Step 4: Determine Measurement Methods and Criteria

How will you be collecting your data? Decisions about the methods and the criteria depend on what you're measuring, the type of data, and maybe on the sample sizes and the frequency of the sampling. You're likely to be using the same methods as you used in earlier Six Sigma phases. If you're collecting attribute data, you'll probably use some form of check sheet. If you're collecting variable data, you may be using calipers, scales, stopwatches, or micrometers

Finally, depending on your measurement system, it may be necessary to conduct a measure/gage analysis study, as discussed in the Measure phase, Chapter 7.

Step 5: Calculate the Parameters of the Control Chart

Collect the data, using the plan that you've developed in steps 3 and 4. You need at least 20 data points to create a control chart. Then, plot the data points on the type of control chart you determined in step 2.

Control Charts—the Basics

A control chart is a graph used to show how a process changes over time. The horizontal axis represents sample numbers or points in time. The vertical axis represents measurements from samples. You plot your data points in chronological order from left to right.

After plotting your data points, you calculate the process average. Then, you draw a horizontal *centerline* to represent that average.

Next, you calculate the upper control limit (UCL) and the lower control limit (LCL), which you will draw above and below the centerline to mark the upper and lower boundaries of acceptability.

As mentioned earlier, as a rule of thumb you need to start with at least 20 points to calculate the control limits, which are called *trial control limits*. The control limits represent +/-3 standard deviations from the mean (centerline). The use of +/-3 standard deviations is the result of decades of observation and analysis by statisticians. At that level, if a process is in control, nearly all the points will fall between +3 sigma and −3 sigma. As long as new points continue to fall within the control limits, the process is assumed to be in control.

> **Control limits** Statistically based limits that indicate the amount of variation expected in a process.

If all the data points fall between the control limits and no systematic behavior is evident, then we conclude that the process was *in control* in the past and that the trial control limits are suitable for controlling the process. If data points fall outside the control limits, the process is considered to be out of control, unstable, and unpredictable.

> **In control** Stable, characteristic of a process whose outputs are within the control limits. A process is in *statistical control* if there is no uncontrolled or special cause variation present.

Figure 10-2 shows a control chart. (It's an X-bar chart, which we'll discuss in a moment.) The data points are plotted, the centerline shows the mean of those points, and the control limits are set at +3 sigma and −3 sigma from the mean.

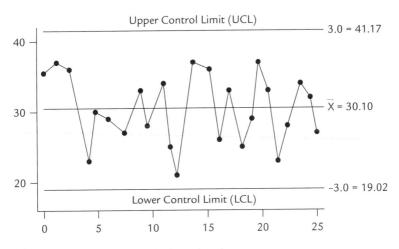

Figure 10-2. Control chart (X-bar chart)

In a process that is in control, any variation is considered *controlled* or *common cause variation*. That means that it occurs naturally and is inherent and expected in a stable process. Common cause variation can be attributed to "chance" or random causes.

> **Common cause** Any factor resulting in variation in a process considered in statistical control.
>
> **Special cause** Any factor resulting in variation in a process considered out of control statistically. Also known as **assignable cause.**

In contrast, in a process that is out of control, variation can also be *uncontrolled* or *special cause variation*. That's variation that occurs when an abnormal action enters a process and produces unexpected and unpredictable results. That underlying source of special cause variation is called an *assignable cause*.

Those are the basic guidelines for control charts in general. Now, let's get more specific.

Control Charts—the Specifics

X-bar, R Chart. The more popular chart used for variable data types is the *X-bar, R chart*. (X-bar, also written with a horizontal line—bar—on top of the X, simply means *average*. R means *range*.) It's used for tracking X and/or Y. The method incorporates two separate charts. The average chart

> **Bar** Indication of a mean, with either the word or a horizontal line on top of a letter, as in X-bar. A mean of means is indicated with a double bar.

tracks the subgroup average from the process and the range chart tracks the range within each subgroup. Putting both charts together allows us to track both the process level and the process variation at the same time, as well as detect the presence of special causes.

Here's a quick example. We're studying the time being wasted in a regional sales office. Figure 10-3 shows the hours not being used on the phone for creating leads.

Figure 10-4 shows the X-bar chart (top, with the centerline "X double bar=50") and the R chart (bottom, with the centerline "R bar=4.65"). With both charts together, we can track process level and process varia-

Week	Hours Wasted	Week	Hours Wasted
1	51	4	51
1	53	4	49
1	56	4	50
1	48	4	55
1	48	4	52
2	51	5	51
2	53	5	65
2	52	5	50
2	51	5	50
2	49	5	48
3	50	6	51
3	49	6	51
3	54	6	50
3	51	6	48
3	53	6	50

Figure 10-3. Wasted time by week, subgroup size = five

tion at the same time and we can detect the presence of any special causes.

You can see that something happened in week 5 that made the process out of control: the data point went above the upper control limit in both charts.

To create this chart:

1. Calculate the average for the subgroup (five data points) for the first week and plot it on the X-bar chart. (A subgroup size of five is a typical industry standard.)

2. Calculate the range for that subgroup by taking the high value minus the low value and plot it on the R chart.

3. Calculate the average and the range for each of the remaining subgroups and plot those points on the charts.

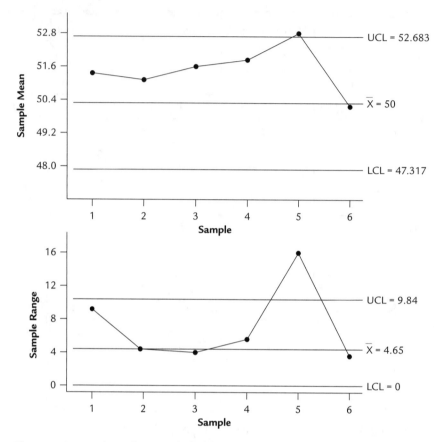

Figure 10-4. X-bar chart and R chart: time wasted

4. Draw a line on both charts at the mean value of the averages (X-bar chart) and the mean value of the ranges (R chart).

5. Calculate the control limits using the formulas in Figure 10-5. Draw those lines on the chart.

6. Interpret the results.

Draw two additional pairs of lines on your control charts: one pair at ±1 sigma from the centerline and another at ±2 sigma. Then use the following subset of rules from the Western Electric Rules (Western Electric, *Statistical Quality Control Handbook,* 1956) to identify out-of-control process problems:

1. One point outside the 3-sigma limit.

Centerline

$$\overline{\overline{x}} = \frac{\sum\limits_{i=1}^{k}\overline{x}_i}{k} \qquad \overline{R} = \frac{\sum\limits_{i}^{k}\overline{R}_i}{k}$$

Control Limits

$$UCL_{\overline{x}} = \overline{\overline{x}} + A_2\overline{R} \qquad UCL_R = D_4\overline{R}$$

$$LCL_{\overline{x}} = \overline{\overline{x}} - A_2\overline{R} \qquad LCL_R = D_3\overline{R}$$

Where:

$\overline{\overline{x}}$ = Average of the subgroup averages, it becomes the centerline of the control chart

$\overline{x}_i$ = Average of each subgroup

k = Number of subgroups

R_i = Range of each subgroup (maximum observation – minimum observation)

$\overline{R}$ = Average range of the subgroups, the centerline on the range chart

$UCL_{\overline{x}}$ = Upper control limit on average chart

$LCL_{\overline{x}}$ = Lower control limit on average chart

UCL_R = Upper control limit on the range chart

LCL_R = Lower control limit on the range chart

A_2, D_3, D_4 = Constants that vary according to subgroup sample size

Subgroup Size	A_2	D_3	D_4
2	1.880	—	3.267
3	1.023	—	2.574
4	0.729	—	2.282
5	0.577	—	2.114
6	0.483	—	2.004
7	0.419	0.076	1.924
8	0.373	0.136	1.864
9	0.337	0.184	1.816
10	0.308	0.223	1.777

Figure 10-5. Formulas for calculating centerline and control limits for X-bar and R charts

2. Two of three consecutive points outside the 2-sigma limit and on the same side.

3. Four of five consecutive points outside the 1-sigma limit and on the same side.

4. Eight consecutive points on one side of the centerline.

> **Don't Use Spec Limits Instead of Control Limits**
>
> Some people discuss control limits and specification limits as if they could be used in the same ways. That's wrong: the concepts and the values are completely different—and there's usually no relationship between them.
>
> Spec limits, as we explained in Chapter 7, represent customer requirements: they show the limits past which outputs are unacceptable. Control limits represent process behavior: they show how much variation there can be in outputs. In short, spec limits show what we want and don't want; control limits show what we've got.

X-Bar and Sigma Chart. A variation on the X-bar and R chart is the *X-bar and sigma chart*. This chart is used with processes for which the subgroup size is 11 or more. The X-bar and sigma chart is also used to monitor the effects of process improvement theories. Instead of charting variability using subgroup range, it uses subgroup standard deviation, which uses each individual reading and therefore measures the process spread more effectively.

Xi Chart. Another control chart for analyzing variable data is the *Xi chart,* also known as *X chart* or *individual* chart. The Xi chart is similar to the X-bar chart except that it plots for a sample size of one and it is usually used with a *moving range chart*, rather than the simple R chart used with the X-bar chart. Confused?

Xi and moving range charts are generally used when it's not possible to use rational subgroups for measurements, when it's more convenient to track observations individually rather than with subgroup averages, or when the process distribution is very non-normal (skewed—asymmetrical on either side of the mean—or bounded on one or both sides—not tapered). Each measurement (a subgroup of one) consists of one observation. The data points are plotted according to a time-based X-axis, in the sequence in which the process generated the data. The moving range chart used with the Xi chart plots the range between each data point and the point immediately preceding it.

P Chart. The *P chart* (P for *proportion*) is a control chart for attribute data. The P chart measures the proportion of defective items in a subgroup (number of defectives per subgroup size). Data collection worksheets for a P chart would show the number of total items in each subgroup and the number of defectives for each. The P chart is generally more applicable to more processes.

The method for creating a P chart is very similar to the method used for the X-bar, R chart, except there are different formulas for calculating the control limits. With attribute data control charts, it's possible that the calculated LCL will be a negative number; in that case there is actually no lower control limit.

Here are the basic equations for the P chart:

Centerline: $\bar{p} = \dfrac{\text{total number of defective items}}{\text{total number of items inspected}}$

Control limits:

$$UCL_p = \bar{p} + 3\sqrt{\dfrac{\bar{p}(1-\bar{p})}{n_i}}$$

$$LCL_p = \bar{p} - 3\sqrt{\dfrac{\bar{p}(1-\bar{p})}{n_i}}$$

Where:

$\bar{p}$ is the average proportion of defective (nonconforming) items

n_i is the number inspected in each subgroup

UCL_p is the upper control limit on the P chart

LCL_p is the lower control limit on the P chart

Since the control limits are a function of sample size, they will vary for each sample but will be constant when the sample size is constant. It is a good practice to fix the sample size in order to simplify the interpretation of the chart.

Here's an example. A project is intended to shorten the time required to close insurance claims. The cycle time of the adjuster's reports have been determined to be a critical X to overall cycle time. Completed reports for each day are checked and the cycle time for each is recorded. Reports taking longer than three days are considered to be defects. The key is knowing the practical definition of the defect. Since the reports are either good or bad and the number of reports processed in a day will vary, a P chart will can be used (Figure 10-6).

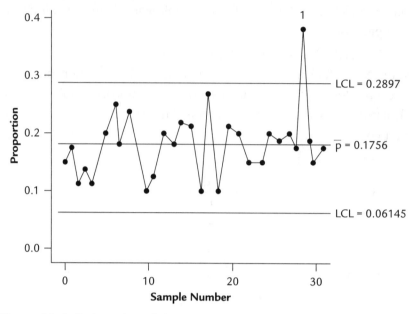

Figure 10-6. P chart: late claims reports

The rules for detecting out-of-control conditions for the P-chart are the following:

1. One point outside the 3-sigma limit.

2. Nine points in a row on the same side of the centerline.

3. Six points in a row, all increasing or all decreasing.

4. 14 points in a row alternating up and down.

If there were any points below the lower control limit, indicating exceptionally short times, that would call for special attention in setting possible best practices.

Always attempt to understand why the quality was so much better within a subgroup than standard. This type of process knowledge could prove invaluable in achieving a permanent process improvement.

NP Chart. An NP chart is similar to the P chart, with two differences. It is used to track attribute data in terms of numbers rather than proportions. All the subgroups must be the same size.

C Chart. A C chart (count) is used to track attribute data in terms of counts per subgroup. All subgroups must be the same size.

U Chart. A U chart (unit) is used to track *attribute data* in terms of counts per unit of a subgroup. Subgroups can be any sizes.

Step 6: Develop a Control Plan

At this point, you should develop a *control plan* to ensure that the process stays in control and that changes are maintained for the long term. In other words, to sustain the gain.

A control plan contains control charts, of course, but a control plan consists of much more. The control plan is one of the foundations of the DMAIC process. In fact, it is one thing that differentiates Six Sigma projects from traditional projects. Control plans provide a written description of the actions required at each phase of the process to keep all process inputs and outputs in control. The components include the following:

1. Training plans
   - what kinds of training to provide to which people

2. Process documentation
   - procedures for process setup
   - process flowcharts documenting the current best practices

3. Monitoring procedures
   - what, where, and when to monitor to maintain the best performance levels
   - target performance levels for critical steps
   - SPC charts as appropriate, prescribing which chart to use for each process metric and how and when to collect the data

4. Response plan
   - trouble-shooting guidelines: what signals to watch out for
   - procedures to follow when there is a signal of failure (out-of-control points on control charts, non-random behavior within control limits, conditions and/or variables proven to produce defects present in the process, check sheet failure, automation failure, etc.)

5. Institutionalization plan

  – what steps will be taken to ensure that the current procedures are used consistently

  – how the process operators and owner will identify and confirm future improvements

The plans must be complete enough to ensure that the process owners and operators can maintain a high level of process performance over time and especially the gains achieved by the Six Sigma team. Much of the key information can be depicted graphically, as in the example in Figure 10-7.

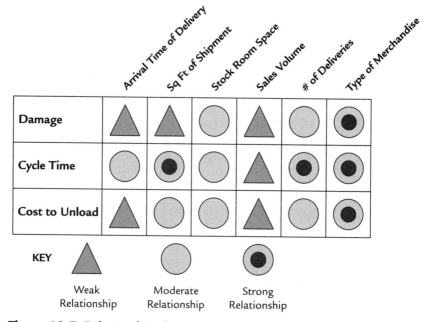

Figure 10-7. Relationships between input measures and output measures

Control plans are living documents, maintained and updated throughout the lifecycle of a process. Updates are made as measurement and processing systems are improved. Control plans do not replace detailed operator instructions, but only describe how the process will be controlled. When the control plan is completed, the process owners will have a new process, with improved performance and minimal risk of

---

Prepare for Failures

Failure Modes and Effects Analysis (FMEA) can also be a useful analysis and documentation tool here, especially where responses to individual failure modes are prescribed. FMEA is especially useful when risks are high. It is a disciplined methodology for identifying potential failures and planning to prevent them. You think through all the possible ways in which a process can fail. Then you rank the frequency, severity, and impact of each failure. Finally, you develop countermeasures for those that would cause the most trouble to you or your customers.

---

future deterioration of performance (at least relative to the defect that has been fixed).

The creation of the control plan is the culmination of learning that has taken place over the course of the DMAIC process. Effective control plans must be simple to implement and easily communicated to the solution team. The intent of an effective control plan strategy is to operate processes consistently, on target, with minimum variation, and minimizing process tampering (over-adjustment) and to ensure that the process improvements become institutionalized, "the way we do it."

The sample checklist (Figure 10-8) for a manufacturing environment can serve as a guide for creating a checklist for a control plan appropriate for your business.

Step 7: Train the People and Use the Charts

The final step in the Control phase is to train the necessary people and to implement and analyze the control charts. The training should follow the requirements specified in your control plan. It should enable the process operators and owner to monitor the process by maintaining and analyzing control charts.

Generally, the effective use of any control chart will require periodic revision of the control limits and centerlines. Some practitioners set regular periodic reviews and revisions of control chart limits, such as every week, every month, or every 25, 50, or 100 samples.

Control Plan Items	Check Off
Process maps detail manufacturing steps, material flow, and important variables	☐
Key product or process variables identified with importance to customer, desired target value, and specification range defined	☐
Long- and short-term capability trend charts track variation reduction process	☐
Key and critical input variables identified with targets, statistically determined control limits, and control strategies defined	☐
Reaction plan in place for out-of-spec material	☐
Measurement systems are capable with calibration requirements specified	☐
Sampling, inspection, and testing plans include how often, where, and to whom results reported	☐
Maintenance schedules and product segregation requirements	☐
Training materials describe all aspects of process operation and responsibilities	☐
Documentation standards met if required	☐
Process improvement efforts fully documented and available for reference	☐
Control plan is reviewed and updated quarterly and resides in the operating area	☐

Figure 10-8. Control plan checklist: example

The control chart limits are a critical part of SPC. The centerline of a control chart must always show average of the plotted points, regardless of what statistic is plotted. The upper control limit (UCL) and the lower control limit (LCL) should be set at the conventional distance of ±3 standard deviations from the centerline.

As mentioned earlier, a process is in control when the data points fall within the bounds of the control limits

> **Find out More**
> If you want to know more about SPC, I recommend reading *Business Statistics Demystified* by Steven M. Kemp and Sid Kemp.

> **"In Control" Is Not Necessarily "Acceptable"**
> When a process is in control, it means only that the performance is stable and predictable. It does *not* mean that the performance is acceptable to you or your customers. If the average of an in-control process is off target from where you want it to be or the control limits are too far apart (meaning there is too much common cause variation), your only course of action is to make fundamental changes in the process. You need to redesign the process in some way so that there is a different mix of common cause factors.

and the points do not display any nonrandom patterns. A process is in control when only common causes—causes inherent in the process—affect the process output. It is out of statistical control when special causes result in variation. Then an assignable cause must be detected and then controlled. Examples include differences in supplier, shift, or day of the week.

Take a practical approach to SPC. Do not overcontrol the process where it is not cost-effective to do so. Since control limits make it possible to distinguish between common (inherent) and special-cause variation, they give us the means to minimize reaction to variation that is expected (i.e., avoid false alarms) and to not react when the process variation is simply random.

The big challenges will come from setting rules for consequences from out-of-control events. If you *do not* have any consequences, SPC will not work, no matter what the control chart, theory, or method! Consequences can be as simple as reducing the salesperson's incentive for a certain amount of time, making the shipping department triple inspection without pay, or stopping the manufacturing process to fix the problem of shipping bad products to customers. Something is going to happen—but it is *not nothing!*

Pre-control

The simplest form of SPC is a method called pre-control. Pre-control provides quick feedback on the process, working like a traffic light (Figure 10-9). You mark your control chart with specification limits—the upper and lower boundaries of values that are acceptable to the customer, as discussed in Chapter 7. The area between the spec limits is divided into three parts.

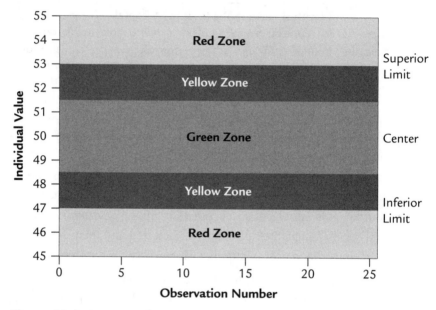

Figure 10-9. Pre-control—a very visual form of SPC

The middle 50 percent is the green zone, the areas on either side of that zone are yellow zones, and the areas beyond the spec limits are red zones.

- If a unit (product or service) of work measures in the green zone, we continue operating the process.

- If a unit measures in either yellow zone, we suspect that an adjustment is needed.

- If two units measure in the same yellow zone, we adjust the process. Then, if two units measure in opposite yellow zones, we conclude that variation has increased significantly and we adjust in the opposite direction.

- If a unit measures in a red zone, we stop the process and take corrective action.

A process is qualified for pre-control when five consecutive units fall in the green region. We must requalify the process after any interruption or restart including modifications to process conditions, change of shifts, setups, etc. If a process is not centered, it is very unlikely that it can be qualified. If a process does not follow a normal distribution, mathematical transformations can be used to make the distribution normal before applying pre-control.

There are five preliminary activities associated with pre-control:

1. Process characterization, which includes calculating the short-term standard deviation (σ_{st})

2. Process improvement (Improve phase)

3. Definition of the pre-control regions

4. Process qualification

5. Process operation

Pre-control Color Usage

The green zone, defined as ±1.5 sigma, covers 86.64 percent of the area within the normal curve. The yellow zones, from 1.5 sigma to 3.0 sigma and from –1.5 sigma to –3.0 sigma, represent 6.55 percent of the area under each tail of the normal curve. The red zones, the regions below mean –3.0 sigma and above mean +3.0 sigma, each contain 0.13 percent of the area under the curve.

There is no rule of thumb to establish the sampling frequency used in pre-control. You must consider factors such as the nature of the process, production volume, and operators' experience.

Pre-control is based on specifications. It is applicable to all areas of business. It can be used in manufacturing processes such as machining, forming, painting, assembly, and in transactional processes such as customer service, order or form filling, invoice collection, etc. You can use it to know that your sales are down or shipping errors are too high.

Step 9: Conduct a Phase-Gate Review

At the end of the Control phase the Black Belt will continue to report to the executive leaders on the status of the project. This presentation is an opportunity for you to ask questions, make suggestions, address any problems, allocate additional resources, provide support, and show your commitment. The phase-gate review at this, like the other stages, continues to ensure that the team stays focused and the project stays on track.

Mistake Proofing

Mistake proofing is typically the last tool of the Control phase to be deployed. The purpose of mistake proofing or error proofing is to determine methods that will ensure that a process will not allow defects. Mistake proofing can be applied to any process with repetitive steps that could be skipped, performed out of order, or not conducted correctly. Mistake proofing ensures that tasks can only be done the right way.

A mistake is any wrong action or statement proceeding from faulty judgment, inadequate knowledge, or inattention. A mistake is an action; a defect is the result. You may have heard the term *poka-yoke*, which is Japanese for a mistake-proofing device. Poka-yoke or mistake proofing helps operators (employees) work more easily and eliminates troubles associated with defects. Even if an operator makes a mistake, poka-yoke measures will prevent a defect from being passed on to the next step in the process. This will further reduce costs by eliminating inspection time.

We're surrounded by mistake proofing. Electric coffee pots have automatic shut-offs, bathroom or outside electric circuits have ground fault interrupter circuit breakers, medicines are sold in tamper-proof packaging and child-proof containers, computers ask, "Are you sure?" after the user selects important operations such as to delete or to close a program, cars and trucks have warning lights and buzzers, and this list could go on and on.

Do you have any processes where any of the following types of mistakes occur?

- Someone forgets to do something, not concentrating.
- Someone misunderstands something and jumps to a conclusion.
- Someone identifies something incorrectly, perhaps viewing it incorrectly, from too far away or too quickly.
- Someone makes errors because of inadequate training.
- Someone ignores the rules.
- Someone gets distracted or tired.
- Someone acts too slowly to make a decision.

- Someone does something wrong because there are no written and visual standards or the standards are insufficient or confusing.

- Someone makes a mistake intentionally.

These should serve as a checklist while mistake-proofing. Try your best to take control over *repetitive* tasks or actions that depend on constantly being alert or on memory. Here are the ten most common errors:

1. Processing omissions

2. Processing errors

3. Error in setting up a workpiece

4. Assembly omissions (missing parts)

5. Inclusion of a wrong part or item

6. Wrong workpiece

7. Operations errors

8. Adjustment, measurement, dimensional errors

9. Error in equipment maintenance

10. Error in preparation of setup or tool adjustments

Part of mistake proofing is to increase visibility—to make all problems visible and to make proper procedures visible. You ideally want to create a workplace where problem points can be recognized at a glance, so that remedial action can be taken immediately. You also want to use visual controls to show how to do the job (standard operations), show how things are used, show where things are stored, control inventory storage levels, show production status, indicate when people need help, identify hazardous areas, and mistake-proof the operation.

Conclusion

In the Control phase, the team works to maintain the changes that it made in the X's in order to sustain the improvements in the Ys. The team must first develop a control plan, which consists of five basic parts: training plan, documentation plan, monitoring plan, response plan, and institutionalization plan.

You, your Champion, the project Sponsor, and Master Black Belt should develop a training plan for the owners and operators of the process. It should include instructions for reading and interpreting control charts, guidance in understanding and using all the documentation on the improved process, and knowing the contingency response plan and how to implement it, if necessary.

With the documentation plan, the project team should ensure that its improvements are institutionalized—that all new process steps, standards, and documentation are integrated into normal operations and that systems, procedures, policies, instructions, and budgets are modified to sustain the gains it has achieved. It is a team effort and responsibility to control the solution that was solved during the DMAIC process.

Summary of the Major Steps in the Control Phase

1. Select the variable to chart.
2. Select the type of control chart to use.
3. Determine rational subgroup size and sampling interval/frequency.
4. Determine measurement methods and criteria.
5. Calculate the parameters of the control chart.
6. Develop a control plan.
7. Train the people and use the charts.
8. Conduct a Phase-Gate Review.

Chapter 11

Sustain Your Six Sigma Gains

"Trying harder" isn't necessarily the solution to achieving more. It may not offer any real promise for getting what you want out of life. Sometimes, in fact, it's a big part of the problem.
—Price Pritchett

Why don't you try something different? Price Pritchett describes a poignant scene in a story in *You2*. On a summer afternoon, while visiting a resort, he noticed a familiar, distressing noise. It was a large housefly flying against the window over and over, using all of its energy trying to escape. The buzzing wings tell the touching anecdote of the fly's strategy: *try harder!* But its strategy—*try harder!*—was not working.

The fly just could not try hard enough to achieve something that was impossible. Nevertheless, it was betting its life on breaking through the glass by just trying harder again and again.

Across the room, ten seconds of flying time, was an open door. It would have taken the fly so little effort to change its strategy and soon be free.

Why, after failing so many times, didn't the fly give up on the window and try a different way out, another strategy? Why was it obsessed with trying again and again something that wasn't working?

Who knows? Unfortunately, the fly would keep on trying until it had no more energy.

Pritchett concludes his story with the quote that started this chapter. Then he adds, "If you stake your hopes for a breakthrough on trying harder than ever, you may kill your chances for success."

Often we achieve more by *trying harder*. However, sometimes that strategy doesn't work. In fact, as we see with this fly and many businesses around us, sometimes trying harder becomes the final strategy, ending only with failure and death.

Don't be the fly! The DMAIC process works. The major focus of process improvement is completing the Measure and Analyze phases. Those phases set the stage for improvement. Hypotheses should come from the people closest to the process being tested, whatever the step or the phase in the DMAIC process. Try these fixes. Your efforts usually will focus on one or two input X's that are suspected to be related to a problem. It's curiosity that drives you to innovative solutions. Constantly ask, "What if we tried this?" Innovation is important and Six Sigma helps us validate our innovative solutions.

Taking Stock

Now that we have reached the last chapter of this book, let's pause to take stock. It is my hope that I have provided you with the information you need to implement a successful Six Sigma initiative within your small business. Perhaps you are in the midst of your implementation or you have completed your first Six Sigma project. Did you realize the results you expected? Did you find hidden sources of revenue? Did you eliminate a defect? Are your customers happier?

Six Sigma is not a temporary fix. It is not something you do just once. Six Sigma should be an ongoing, continuous endeavor for as long as you stay in business! Six Sigma is a way of life. Think about it: why would you train employees, devote considerable resources, expend time, money and effort, and forever change your organizational culture for one single Six Sigma project? What is the best way to get the maximum return on your investment? By sustaining the gains!

It is absolutely vital that you continue the momentum gained from your initial project by picking new projects, creating new teams, committing additional and/or new resources, and continuously improving your business. I would be willing to bet that if your first project has been a success, you can hardly wait to move on to the next one!

Sustaining Is Hard Work

This final chapter will help you sustain the gains of your Six Sigma implementation. To be honest with you, it is not easy. It is not unusual for companies, regardless of their size, to have difficulties with keeping the momentum going. In fact, many organizations fail in their efforts to sustain the gains.

What is the best way to keep Six Sigma alive? Why is it that many organizations can't sustain the gains? Most often because they failed to ensure some key elements.

What Makes a Six Sigma Implementation Successful?

The following elements are absolutely essential to successful implementation of Six Sigma:

1. Consistent and visible leadership involvement.

2. A measurement system to track progress, providing accountability for the initiative.

3. Internal and external benchmarking of the organization's products, services, and processes. You must find out where you *really* are.

4. Setting challenging stretch goals that focus your employees on changing the process, not just tweaking it.

5. Educating and informing every member of your organization about the Six Sigma methodology.

6. Developing the infrastructure to support change throughout your organization.

7. Working to create a "cause," not just a business success.

Six Sigma is your foundation for future success. It is up to you to build on it!

How to Assess Your Progress

Once you have implemented Six Sigma, you should have reached certain milestones that will indicate whether your initiative has been successful. Let's take a look at the first year of your Six Sigma implementation.

Here's what you should accomplish within the first six months. Success with the items on this list is an indication that you are on your way to achieving your Six Sigma goals:

1. A list of problems that will result in savings and growth.

2. A trust in the metrics that drive your business.

3. Three to five percent reduction in waste, resulting in a two to five percent profit savings.

4. Resources focusing on improvement.

5. Open, secure environment to address cost issues.

What's the most efficient way to ensure Six Sigma success? Create an infrastructure to support your implementation. What do I mean? In previous chapters I wrote about integrating Six Sigma into every aspect of your business. Six Sigma must be a part of everything you do within your organization.

Be careful of the self-proclaimed Six Sigma "experts." The rapid and widespread acceptance of Six Sigma and its phenomenal success have sparked a cottage industry, a proliferation of "experts" all claiming to possess the knowledge to put the methodology into action. Results frequently fall short of expectations, however, because while some of the practitioners are authentic, trained by genuine Six Sigma Master Black Belts, others are virtual imposters who do not fully understand or practice the true Six Sigma methodology.

Though what the self-proclaimed "experts" are selling does not have enough substance to yield optimal results, it contains enough information to be dangerous. The intellectual property looks credible enough to fool the non-expert and even generates excitement about Six Sigma implementations. In truth, however, being disseminated now are altered, covered-up, and watered-down versions of the original success model—mechanical, recipe thinking diluted from the true, independent problem solving that once existed, morphed by the knockoffs. Essential tools are being misapplied, resulting in less-than-stellar performances.

How can you avoid making mistakes with "experts" who are not qualified and are incapable of helping your company get the most benefit from Six Sigma? If your company is large enough to take on one or more Six Sigma consultants, here are some criteria you can use to select who you want to work with:

1. True Six Sigma firms will be able to assess upfront the money to be saved with enough confidence to guarantee a minimum savings equal to 20 percent of a company's revenues, accepting the risk of being compensated on the basis of this savings.

2. The average project savings should be $175,000 per project, regardless of industry or size of company.

3. The way that Six Sigma firms bill should give you insight into their main focus. If they bill for training outcomes, then that is what you will get—training. Look for billing based on results.

4. Get three references and speak with not only the corporate champion or company owner, but also the people who worked on the projects.

5. Six Sigma firms must provide a surgical solution that fits your business structure without affecting the results or compromising the DMAIC method.

6. The highest-quality provider is the lowest-cost provider.

Small business leaders first show their commitment to achieve Six Sigma results when they drive resources to solve a problem. Move quickly to line up the resources for the initial projects. This will send the message throughout the organization that things are really going to change.

Case Studies

Let's tie it altogether. Here are three case studies to show briefly how DMAIC works.

Case Study 1

Define: The purchase order placement cycle was too lengthy and would not effectively support a high-volume and repetitive manufacturing program. Current PO placement cycle times often resulted in inefficient allocations of purchasing staff and material deliveries that did not support planned stock dates.

Measure: Since there was no effective data-collection system, the first step was to collect detailed historic records on POs from the previous business year. PO placement cycle time specs were created. Process capability indicated that material was late 23 percent of the time.

Analyze: Pareto charts were created by dollar threshold values. A common problem area among all four categories was the process time from selecting a supplier to actually entering the PO. A hypothesis test was performed to alleviate concern that dollar value thresholds had an impact on PO placement cycle time drivers.

Improve: Review of data and brainstorming pointed to three problems causing long cycle times: buyer workload distribution, lack of a preferred supplier base, and inadequate purchasing software. Work teams were organized to manage buyer workload issues, a preferred/certified supplier program was started, and online procurement forms have been made available.

Control: A management report series has been developed to report monthly on departmental and individual metrics. Performance goals were introduced to buyer annual performance plans.

Results: Overall process capability improved. Average cycle times dropped from 17 days to 11 days. Material deliveries improved from an average of 23 percent late to 16 percent late. Savings was $105,000 annually in decreased buyer staffing requirements.

Case Study 2

Define: Errors were being made in the ordering process; customers were receiving the wrong product or too many products. Administrative processing errors represented 50 percent of the nondefective product returns.

Measure: Members of each functional area were interviewed to understand the ordering process. An attribute gage R&R was conducted at the call center point where customers called for return authorization. Among other things, credit return error codes were allocated to customer returns. The system of allocating codes was found to be deficient. New defect data-collection sheets were introduced and the data was collected and categorized into first and second levels of reasons for return.

Analyze: The categorized data was subject to chi-squared tests to validate data concerning differences by sales region, representatives, and ordering system. (A chi-squared test is any statistical test that results in a chi-square distribution—the sum of the squares of the observed values minus the expected values divided by the expected values—if the null hypothesis is true.) Differences were found to be significant by ordering system.

Improve: Changes were made in the processing of customer orders to check for a range of conditions that resulted in too many products being provided, the main error that the supplier could control.

Control: A simple control system was introduced to review all orders received the previous day. New procedures were introduced for the assignment of credit return error codes at the call center.

Results: In the first 12 weeks after implementation in one sales region, 32 sales orders were identified as duplicates for a total of 139 line items. The company was able to save $308,000 for one sales region annually, representing the value of stock that was produced but not required by customers.

Case Study 3

Define: On average, every order delivered to customers had one component missing (short shipped). Management has directed that the incidence of such short shipments be reduced by 50 percent and thus lessen the administrative burden of coordinating such shipments, increase customer satisfaction, and reduce the risk of losing future sales.

Measure: Over 80 percent of the short shipments were due to one section, the Industrial Division. Of these, only half were "approved short shipments." In other words, the other half of the short shipments were only detected by customers on unpacking or installation. A total of 838 parts or kits had to be shipped later to enable customers to complete installation. There was no formal process in place for managing short shipments.

Analyze: Process maps (graphic representations of a process) and cause-and-effect matrices were developed to identify the key variables (X's) driving the short-shipping results. Chi-squared tests were conducted to test people's beliefs that differences by product groups existed within the Industrial Division. No differences were detected.

Improve: A short-ship process was designed. An FMEA was conducted to identify those factors that could cause this new process to fail. These factors were either fool-proofed or controlled.

Control: System controls were put into place, including a more effective checklist, tagging of the location on the product where missing parts are required, and use of the corporate information system to track the short shipments effectively. Further opportunities were identified in reducing some of the causes of the short shipments that fell outside the scope of this project, e.g., order entry and production scheduling.

Results: The company achieved a 52 percent reduction in additional shipments required to complete an order and $116,000 in direct cost savings in the shipping function, not including soft savings in the retention of customers.

The Six Sigma Epilogue

Customers have critical-to-business expectations. We are in business to achieve a phenomenal customer satisfaction rate that exceeds critical-to-business expectations. We thrive to make profitable *bottom-line results*. We have processes that are repetitive in our business. Our goal is to create knowledge and take action to reduce cycle time, reduce defects, reduce variations, expand, and grow.

We create this knowledge by collecting data, stating the problem in statistical terms such as the mean and standard deviation of the process. We validate the data collected and then analyze it to determined the vital few factors that are the root of the problem. Next, we create a predictable equation or relationship in the process variations to output. Finally, we improve the process, control it, and sustain the gain while always quantifying our bottom-line results. We share our knowledge to ensure that everyone understands and benefits from that knowledge. Then we as an organization achieve our goals, which results in sustained and satisfied internal and external customers.

At this point I could wish you the best of luck in your small business, but luck is not a Six Sigma belief. Luck is not predictable.

> "When we start approaching what we don't know, that is the beginning of the Six Sigma journey."
> —Greg Brue

If you follow the basic methods outlined in this book you will not be lucky, but you can predict your successes. I don't think, feel, or believe that you will be a success, but I am 95 percent confident that you will succeed!

Index